WEAVING IN MINIATURE

by Carol Strickler & Barbara Taggart

1980
Interweave Press, Inc.
Loveland, Colorado 80537

ISBN 0-934026-02-5

LIBRARY OF CONGRESS
CATALOG CARD NO.: 80-80935
Strickler, Carol and Taggart, Barbara

Weaving In Miniature
Loveland, Colorado   Interweave Press, Inc.

CONTENTS

"Strickler Hill Museum", 1' = 1".

INTRODUCTION

INTEREST IN DOLLHOUSES and scale miniatures has boomed in recent years. As this interest has matured, there has been an increased attention to accuracy and authenticity of details such as the textiles used in a miniature home or setting. Concurrently with this boom in miniatures there has been a trend among some weavers toward use of finer threads and loom-controlled weaves to produce fine fabrics.

In this monograph we bring together those two interests of dollhouse-furnishing and "small-minded" weaving. The instructions and drafts are designed to be used by an experienced loom-weaver to create textiles in miniature scale (primarily 1"/1') for authentic dollhouse interiors or other small projects.

A NOTE about the drafting methods used in this book:

Threading and profile drafts read from right to left. Treadlings and drawdowns read from bottom to top, since that is the way fabric builds on the loom. Profile or block drafts are represented by filled-in squares in the threading and by solidly-filled areas in the drawdown. Thread-by-thread drafts use numbers (indicating shafts or harnesses) in the threading, a sinking-shed tie-up, and, in the drawdown, horizontal lines to indicate the paths of the wefts as they cross over the warps that are lowered by the treadling. This method gives a drawdown which accurately pictures the fabric (an interlacement of lines). Where the standard treadling (each pattern shot followed by a tabby shot) is used, the tabby threads are "understood" and are not shown in the drawdown.

Any deviations from these standard drafting methods will be indicated in the text or draft-captions. A weaver using the drafts on a rising-shed loom should simply use the opposite tie-up from that given (that is, *raise* the shafts that are *not* lowered in the sinking-shed drawdown). The fabric will then weave face up.

A NOTE about the fabrics and illustrations:

All miniature fabrics were designed and woven by Carol Strickler and Barbara Taggart unless otherwise indicated. All photographs are by Carol Strickler unless otherwise indicated.

MINIATURIZATION OF A FABRIC — GENERAL

It is possible to adapt many weaving techniques to the creation of miniature textiles. It is impossible, however, with full-scale fingers and equipment, to weave some fabrics in true miniature scale. To do so, the threads would have to be impractically fine and closely set, and the characteristics of the weave would be lost in the fineness. For example, a 24 ends per inch (EPI) overshot coverlet in true 1"/1' scale would require 288 EPI of cobweb-fine warp, and a ½" pattern block reduced to 1/12 of its original size would be difficult to see. Therefore it is better to change the drafts and weave fabrics that *appear* to be in scale.

One way to weave small things is to use fine threads and small drafts. The thread could be size 20/2 linen, 20/3 or 24/3 cotton, size 40 or 50 or 60 sewing thread, Maypole "Willamette" or other fine wool. Sett could be between 24 and 60 EPI. The pattern draft should be one which has no long skips or large blocks, and which has relatively short repeats. "Rosepath" is an obvious choice which meets these criteria. Other suitable patterns can be found in *Miniature Patterns for Hand Weaving* by Josephine Estes or in *The Bertha Grey Hayes Miniature Patterns* published in the *Shuttle Craft Guild Bulletin* in August and September, 1956. (Figure 1.)

In addition to small overshot patterns, other weaves such as warp-faced and weft-faced plainweave, log cabin,

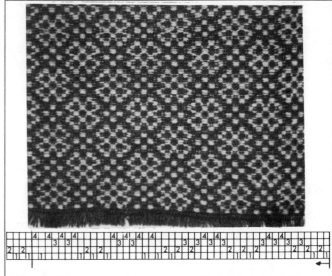

A Bertha Hayes overshot pattern called "Domino". Woven using perle cotton at 30 EPI, with fine wool wefts.
_____ FIGURE 1 _____

honeycomb, summer-and-winter, and some of the pile rug weaves can easily be produced in miniature.

For the weaver who wants more than just a small allover pattern, this monograph will offer another way, that of draft miniaturization. The weaver should be able to produce textiles that closely resemble the originals, and to rewrite drafts to suit miniature use.

COVERLETS

COVERLETS: INTRODUCTION

THE MOST DISTINCTIVE early American textile which can be woven in miniature is a coverlet. Handwoven bed coverlets were common in ordinary American homes from before the Revolutionary War in the 18th century until after the mid-19th century. Even when they were replaced in use by the fancier Jacquard-loom patterned coverlets, the handwoven ones continued to appear in homes, sometimes separated into panels and used as portiere pairs, sometimes cut up and used as curtain linings or mattress pads, often simply retired to the attic as "old-fashioned, but too good to throw out". Woven in the eastern United States and Canada, coverlets of both types traveled west with the settlers. In some regions of the country (primarily the Southern Highlands), coverlets continued to be woven and used as bed covers into the 20th century. The third quarter of the 20th century has seen a strong revival of interest in the coverlets (both handwoven and Jacquard), and such textiles are turning up in attics, estate sales, antique shops and auctions, and museum exhibits.

Because of this history, a miniature handwoven coverlet would be an authentic textile to have in the bedroom or attic of almost any American period dollhouse (except a "wealthy Colonial" one), as well as in a miniature antique shop, covered wagon, frontier cabin or "soddy", etc.

The most common weave used for home-woven coverlets was 4-shaft overshot. A few were made in a 2-shaft weft-face technique, and blankets were usually plainweave or twill. The professional weavers (including a few itinerants) usually had more complex looms, and could create the 6-shaft summer-and-winter, 16-shaft double twill and doubleweave, and other more elaborate coverlets. After the introduction of the Jacquard punched-card mechanism to America in the late 1820's, many professional weavers converted their looms and wove fancy patterns with yarn provided by the buyer. The use of handspun linen for the warp was almost entirely given up when machine-spun cotton became readily and cheaply available after about 1810. So most old coverlets are handspun wool pattern weft on a cotton ground. The wool is usually dark blue (indigo dye) or brick red (madder dye), although many other vegetal dyes were used, especially in the overshot coverlets.

The next chapters will explore some of the possibilities of weaving miniature coverlets with an authentic look.

COVERLETS: OVERSHOT

In the full-scale overshot weave, pattern threads "overshoot" and "undershoot" a plainweave ground fabric. The pattern has three textures formed by blocks of overshots, areas where the pattern weft interweaves 1/1 alongside the tabby weft ("incidentals"), and blocks of plainweave fabric where the pattern wefts "undershoot". The fabric is usually woven using a white or light smooth thread such as cotton for the warp, the same or a slightly smaller thread for the plainweave or "tabby" weft, and a heavier, softer, colored thread such as wool for the pattern weft. Each shot of pattern weft on a pattern shed is followed by a shot of tabby weft on one of the plainweave sheds (which alternate). The warp sett is usually one that will weave a 50/50 (balanced) plainweave in the background.

Full-scale overshot is usually a four-block pattern threaded on four shafts. If the "A" block of the pattern is threaded on shafts 1 and 2 alternately, the "B" block can be threaded on 2 and 3, the "C" block on 3 and 4, and the "D" block on 1 and 4. The more times the use of one pair of shafts is repeated in succession, the wider the overskips of pattern weft will be at that place in the fabric. *Blocks* usually follow each other in twill order (A, B, C, D, A, etc.) and the twill may reverse on any block (A, B, A, B, C, D, C, B, C, etc.). In order to have a perfect plainweave (1-3 vs. 2-4) possible on the threading, odd-numbered and even-numbered shafts must always be used alternately in the threading (Figure 2).

The characteristic appearance of familiar overshot patterns depends on the order and relative sizes of the four blocks. Any full-sized overshot pattern can be reduced to miniature. The pattern blocks will not extend as far and the

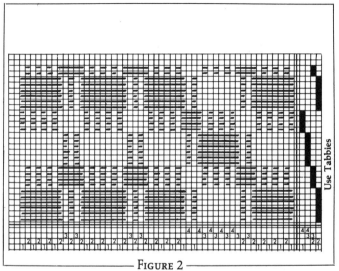

FIGURE 2

skips will be shorter. To look like the original, the blocks must occur in the same order and they must be joined in the same way, but large blocks can be drafted as 2, 3, or 4 thread skips and small blocks can be eliminated.

A pattern block of 1, 2, 1, 2, can be reduced simply to 1, 2. An 8-thread block can be reduced to 4. A 9-thread block can become a 5-thread block. Blocks with an even number of threads must continue to have even numbers and blocks with odd numbers must remain odd numbered. Also,

5

3a. "Lee's Surrender" (315 threads including 2 borders)

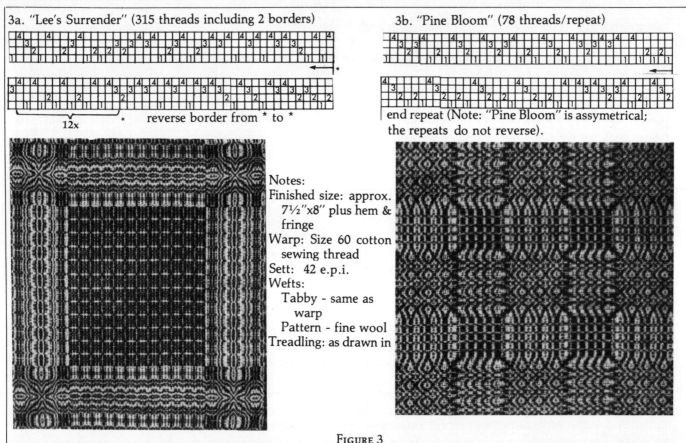

12x   *   reverse border from * to *

3b. "Pine Bloom" (78 threads/repeat)

end repeat (Note: "Pine Bloom" is assymetrical;
the repeats do not reverse).

Notes:
Finished size: approx.
    7½"x8" plus hem &
    fringe
Warp: Size 60 cotton
    sewing thread
Sett: 42 e.p.i.
Wefts:
    Tabby - same as
        warp
    Pattern - fine wool
Treadling: as drawn in

FIGURE 3
Some Additional Miniaturized Overshots

3c. Whig Rose/Lover's Knot

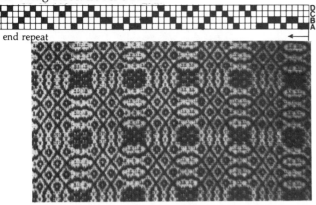

end repeat

3d. "Catalpa Flower" (56 threads/repeat)

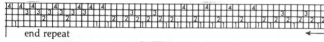

end repeat

blocks that have been reduced should begin and end on the same harness as the larger block.

The number of times the pattern is repeated is completely optional and depends on the number of warp ends the weaver plans to use. An overshot coverlet approximately 7″ wide will have 420 warp ends if it is set at 60 EPI. At 45 EPI there will be 315. An ideal draft is one which will weave between 5 and 10 repeats across the width, possibly with a border at both sides and on the bottom.

Figure 3 shows miniature drafts and coverlets which were derived from full sized overshot pattern drafts. The "Lee's Surrender With Blooming Leaf Border" is reduced from threading drafts in Davison's *Handweaver's Pattern Book*. The "Pine Bloom" is from Burnham's *"Keep Me Warm One Night"*. The "Whig Rose and Lover's Knot" was taken in profile form from several photographs of this design, and the "Catalpa Flower" was taken from a full-sized profile draft of a coverlet.

It is possible to reproduce a tiny replica of a full size coverlet, perhaps a family heirloom or one from a museum collection. Specifically, there are four steps to the entire miniaturization procedure, although shortcuts can sometimes be taken by eliminating one or two of the steps. The four steps are:

1. translation of the original threading draft into its block or profile draft,
2. reduction of the profile draft to minimum size,
3. translation of the reduced profile into a miniature overshot threading, and
4. doing a drawdown of the new threading to test it.

An example of these four steps is shown in Figure 4. In this example, the original 19th-century "Small Sunrise" pattern overshot coverlet (a) has been analyzed, and the full threading draft (b) derived from it. In Step 1, this threading draft is translated into profile form (b), using A for the block on shafts 1-2, B for 2-3, C for 3-4, and D for 1-4. If such fabric analysis and reduction to block form are unfamiliar exercises, instructions can be found in *Designing and Drafting for Handweavers* by Berta Frey, as well as in a few other weaving manuals.

Step 2 is the reduction of the profile draft to a minimum size (Figure 4c). In this case, the reduction was made partly by eliminating all blocks except those necessary to keep the characteristic appearance of the "sunrise" and "table" figures, and partly by reducing the remaining blocks to a simple relationship of "large" (two repeats) and "small" (one repeat). Although the relative sizes of different blocks are usually more varied and complex in a full-sized draft, the simpler relationships (with no block longer than three repeats) are usually necessary in miniatures.

8

Detail of original coverlet, "Small Sunrise".

Miniature Reduction, detail.

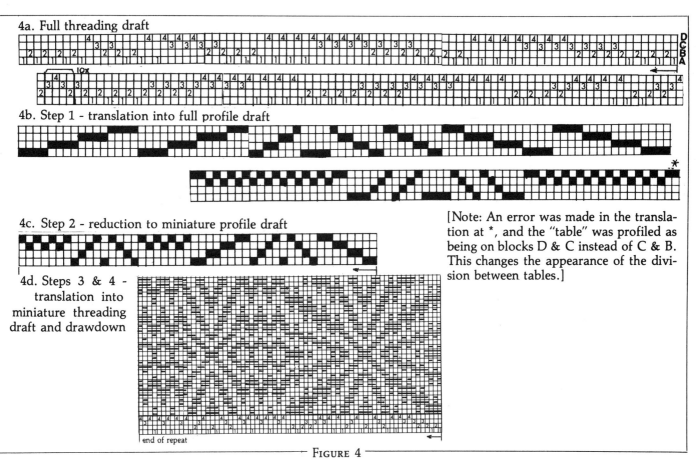

4a. Full threading draft

4b. Step 1 - translation into full profile draft

4c. Step 2 - reduction to miniature profile draft

4d. Steps 3 & 4 - translation into miniature threading draft and drawdown

end of repeat

[Note: An error was made in the translation at *, and the "table" was profiled as being on blocks D & C instead of C & B. This changes the appearance of the division between tables.]

FIGURE 4

In Step 3, the reduced profile is translated into a miniature overshot draft (Figure 4d). This is accomplished by using the same pairs of shafts for blocks (A = 1-2, B = 2-3, C = 3-4, and D = 1-4). A 2-thread or 3-thread skip is drafted for each "small" block of the profile, and a 4-thread or 5-thread skip is drafted for each "large" block. It is important, during this step, to follow the usual drafting "rules" for twill and overshot: odd-numbered and even-numbered shafts must always alternate; blocks which are progressing in a twill order will each contain an even number of warp threads (2 or 4), and blocks on which the direction of the twill reverses will each contain an odd number of warp threads (3 or 5); each block "overlaps" its previous and succeeding block by one thread (i.e. each block shares a thread with adjacent blocks on either side); etc.

Step 4 is the drawdown of the new threading (Figure 4d). This reduced pattern has a 68-thread repeat, which means that use of size 60 sewing thread for warp at a sett of 42 EPI results in 4½ repeats across the width of an approximately 7½" coverlet warp. In this miniature coverlet (Figure 4), the same Size 60 thread was used for tabby weft, and Maypole "Williamette" wool was a suitable pattern weft to weave the blocks squared at the 42 EPI sett. The miniature coverlet copies the colors (blocks dark blue and brick red, alternately) of the original for an authentic look.

10

The original coverlets were usually approximately 65" to 80" wide (woven in two panels, and seamed down the center) and about 84" to 110" long. Top edges were rarely fringed (usually narrowly hemmed, to lie smoothly under the pillows and shams). Bottom edges were either hemmed or fringed, and tape-woven fringe was sometimes applied to the bottom and both sides. Because of this, an average size of about 6½" x 8" is suitable for a miniature coverlet; the resulting fabric will fit many of the old-style miniature beds.

Weft threads should be used that will weave a balanced or slightly elongated weave at whatever sett is used. One of the authors has used size 50 polyester sewing thread at 60 EPI successfully with a 30 dent reed.

The other author has used size 60 (finer) mercerized cotton sewing thread at 42 and 45 EPI in a 15-dent reed with no problems; those warps were used on a large 42" floor loom whose heavy beat would have been disastrous to the warp if any closer sley had been used.

Treadling an overshot pattern "as drawn in" means weaving the blocks in order, as they appear in the draft. Raising shafts 3-4 weaves the A block (threaded on 1-2), raising shafts 1-4 weaves B, etc. Each block should be repeated until it is square or slightly elongated. Care should always be taken to treadle an even number of pattern shots for any block on which the twill direction of the treadling reverses; if the approaching blocks require an odd number of pattern picks, a balancing odd number must be used on the other side of the reversal. If this rule is not followed, the alternating tabbies will not always fall between pattern pairs in the same way, and the pattern will look "wrong" (particularly in the miniature overshot).

Weavers who are not as concerned with authentic reproduction of originally-old coverlet patterns may wish to weave miniature overshot by making their own creative combinations of typical elements. These elements, such as stars, roses, tables, wheels, etc., can be drafted in miniature, and can be used in new combinations by following the drafting rules for miniature overshot. Figures 5 and 6 show several such elements in full-sized and miniature draft and drawdown forms. The profile drafts and drawdowns in Figure 7 suggest some combinations of elements.

The miniature coverlet in Figure 8b is woven from such a combined draft (size 50 sewing thread at 60 EPI), and differs from the full-sized coverlet in Figure 8c only in minor details. Figure 8d shows the same miniature draft, treadled "rose fashion", and Figure 8e shows a full-sized coverlet from which it could have been derived.

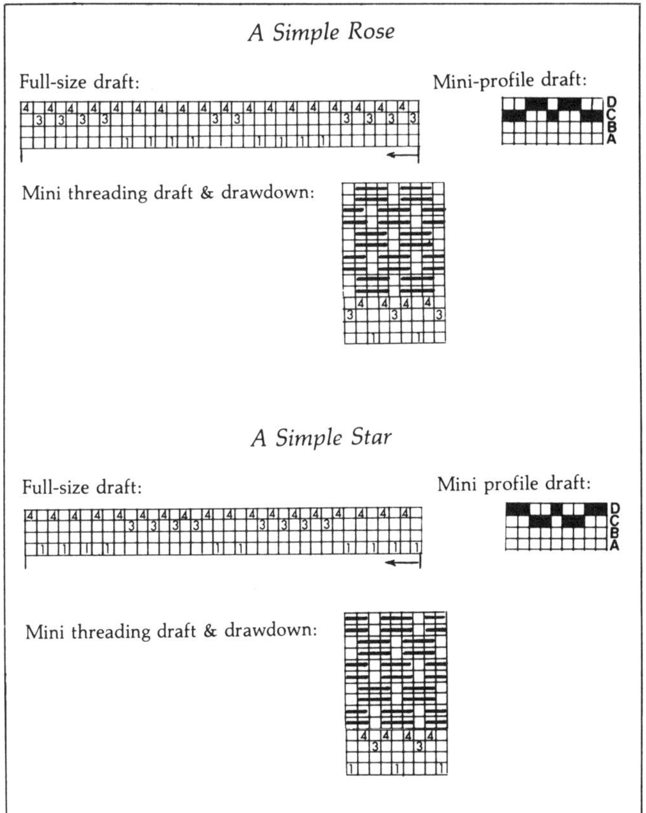

FIGURE 5
Overshot Elements — Miniaturized

11

A Table "Drafted on Opposites":

A full-size draft: Mini profile draft:

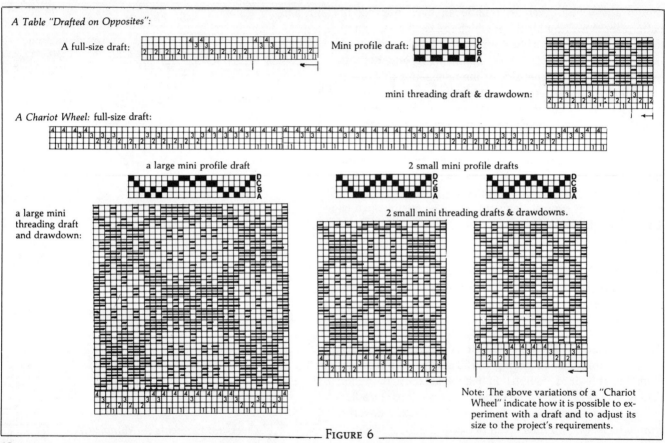

mini threading draft & drawdown:

A Chariot Wheel: full-size draft:

a large mini profile draft   2 small mini profile drafts

a large mini
threading draft
and drawdown: 2 small mini threading drafts & drawdowns.

Note: The above variations of a "Chariot
Wheel" indicate how it is possible to ex-
periment with a draft and to adjust its
size to the project's requirements.

FIGURE 6

Errata

Page 18

Compare with the tie-up on page 20 for the differences in the tied and non-tied effects.

Page 62

2   weave with *dark* (background) weft
4   weave with *dark* (background) weft
     REMOVE STICK

2-4 pick up *background* threads

Page 67

Combination

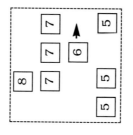

Page 72

insert TAKE OUT STICK   between steps 2 & 3

Page 103

Replace bottom two rows of tie-up with:

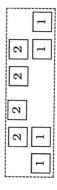

This is gummed paper. Just mosten and affix to the designated page.

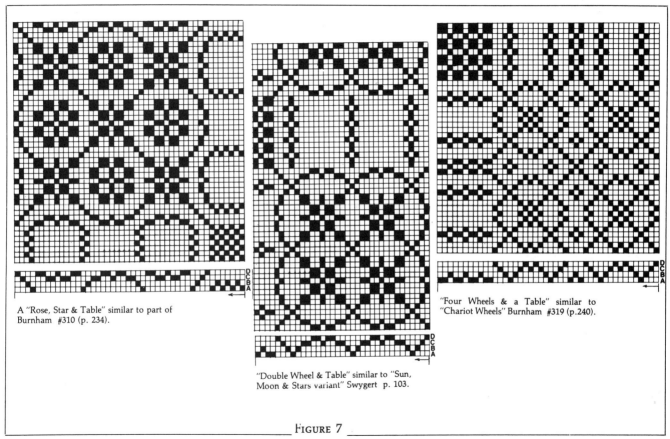

A "Rose, Star & Table" similar to part of Burnham #310 (p. 234).

"Double Wheel & Table" similar to "Sun, Moon & Stars variant" Swygert p. 103.

"Four Wheels & a Table" similar to "Chariot Wheels" Burnham #319 (p.240).

FIGURE 7

8a. A miniature draft combining the star and table elements: (116 threads per repeat)

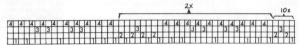

8b. Part of a miniature coverlet woven on the draft. This could pass for a miniature reproduction of the "Nine Stars and Table" full-sized coverlet at 8c.

8c.

8d. The same draft, treadled "rose fashion":

8e. A full-sized "Nine Snowball" or "Dogtrack" coverlet from which the miniature pattern could have been derived:

FIGURE 8

Monk's Belt is a form of overshot weave which uses only two opposite blocks. The technique can be used on any miniature overshot threading draft, by weaving one of the blocks (on a plainweave ground) until square and then weaving the opposite block (on a plainweave ground) until square. Figure 9 shows a drawdown of the Monk's Belt type treadlings on the "Catalpa Flower" miniature overshot draft from Figure 3d.

A second way of weaving Monk's Belt is to design a draft especially for it. The profile draft should be a 2-block design, with blocks of a regular "large and small" relationship such as 2-to-1 or 3-to-1. The profile may be derived from an overshot coverlet of the "Patch" or 2-block types. Figure 10 shows such a full-sized coverlet, "Cloudless Beauty", with 2-block miniature profile and threading drafts derived from it.

The standard method of drafting Monk's Belt type overshot is to thread shafts 1 and 2 alternately for block A, and shafts 3 and 4 alternately for block B. As in overshot, the standard method of weaving is to follow each shot of pattern with a shot of tabby, tabbies alternating. The same type and balance of threads are used as in standard overshot. When a profile draft being translated into Monk's Belt involves 3 or more consecutive repeats of a block, care should be taken to divide that large area and tie down the weft at intervals no greater than 6 threads (see Figures 10b and 10c).

Figure 11a shows a Monk's Belt draft which was designed with a 3-to-1 relationship of block sizes and a large central area with border. The threading draft is also given in Figure 11b. Treadling this Monk's Belt draft in the standard fashion (squared blocks of skips, with each pattern shot followed by a tabby shot) weaves the miniature coverlet shown in Figure 11c.

Other treadlings are possible on a Monk's Belt type threading. One method, treadling "on opposites" with no tabby weft, yields a miniature coverlet very similar in appearance to the unusual 2-block 2-shaft weft-faced coverlets illustrated in Burnham, "Keep Me Warm One Night", #231-234 (pp. 172-173).

Treadling on opposites uses no tabby weft (see Figure 12a). Instead, each pattern shot is followed by a pattern shot of contrasting color on the opposite shed (i.e., 1-2 in dark weft is followed by 3-4 in light). If the yarns are the proper size for the warp sett, this will weave a weft-faced fabric. The miniature coverlet in Figure 12b was woven in this manner on the warp of Figure 11.

The "on opposites" treadling method can also be used on any miniature overshot threading, although the large and small blocks of skips may not be as uniformly related in size. Summer-and-winter threadings may also be treadled "on opposites" to give 2-block weft-faced patterns which will have a 3-to-1 relationship of block size (see "Coverlets: Summer-and-Winter" beginning on p. 24).

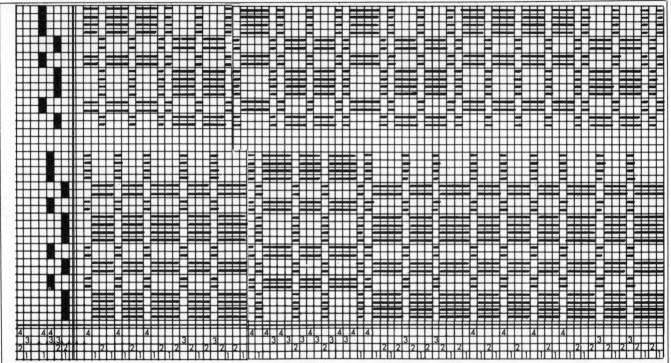

tie-up
(sinking
shed)

Threading

"Monk's Belt" or *"Patch"* treadlings on a miniature overshot threading for *"Catalpa Flower".*

FIGURE 9

10a. "Cloudless Beauty" overshot coverlet, 2 opposite blocks.

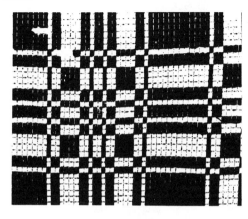

10b. A miniature 2-block profile draft derived from 10a.

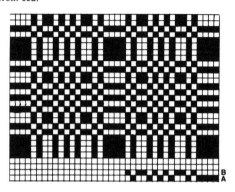

10c. A threading interpretation of profile draft 10b.

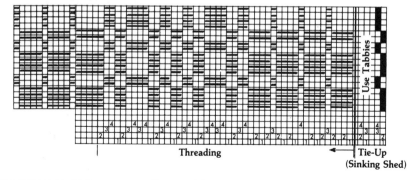

Use Tabbies

Threading

Tie-Up
(Sinking Shed)

FIGURE 10

17

11a. Profile draft for a miniature Monk's Belt coverlet:

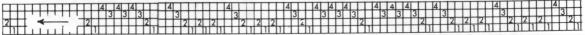

11b. Threading draft for profile 11a.

Warp=24/3 white cotton
Sett=30 e.p.i.
Wefts=A fine white thread and Maypole "Willamette" wool in red and dark blue. Block A is woven in dark blue and block B in red pattern wefts.

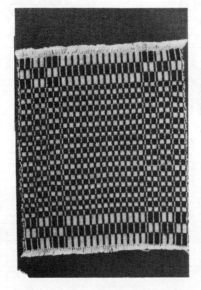
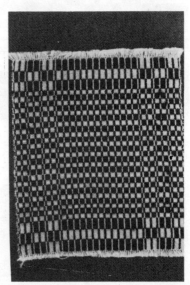

————— FIGURE 11 —————

COVERLETS: HONEYCOMB

Honeycomb is a weave which may use a draft especially designed for it or may be woven as a treadling variation on some other "Monk's Belt" or overshot threadings. The true honeycomb weave has "cells" of plainweave fabric outlined by heavier weft threads which weave plainweave across the entire fabric and outline the cells (Figure 13a). The warp is usually sett to weave *balanced* plainweave in the cells.

A draft threaded for honeycomb will use 2 opposite blocks, just as the Monk's Belt and "Patch" patterns do. Blocks may vary in width, although blocks should not be too wide because the cell wefts will skip across the back of the fabric behind the cells which are not weaving. These skips make the fabric non-reversible.

The standard treadling for honeycomb is to weave each cell by alternating the individual shafts of that cell while holding up the shafts of the other cells, then outline the cells, then weave the next cells. For example: if the pattern is a 2-block design, with the A block threaded on shafts 1 and 2 and the B block on shaft 3 and 4, the standard treadling (*rising* shed) would be:

1-3	heavy thread "outline"
2-4	
1-3-4 ⎫	repeated as desired with finer thread, to square
2-3-4 ⎭	the A-block cell
1-3	heavy thread "outline"
2-4	
1-2-4 ⎫	repeated as desired with finer thread, to square
1-2-3 ⎭	the B-block cell
1-3	
2-4	etc.

The original old coverlets woven in honeycomb were primarily a product of the southeastern United States, and are now often displayed on four-poster beds in Southern mansion reconstructions. They were usually woven entirely in white cotton, using the standard fine thread for warp and cell weft, and a heavier floss or plied thread for the undulating outline weft. These white coverlets were suitable for the hotter weather of the South, since they were usually cotton (not wool) and were a lighter-weight weave than some of the Northern products.

Figure 13b shows a miniature honeycomb coverlet woven on the "Monk's Belt" threading of Figures 11 and 12. It differs from the standard honeycomb by not having

19

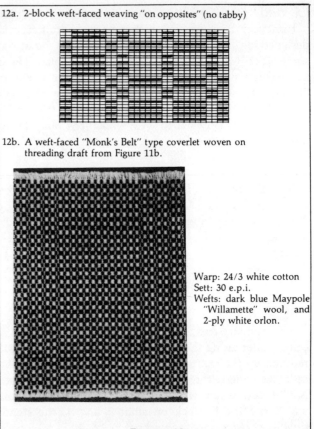

12a. 2-block weft-faced weaving "on opposites" (no tabby)

12b. A weft-faced "Monk's Belt" type coverlet woven on threading draft from Figure 11b.

Warp: 24/3 white cotton
Sett: 30 e.p.i.
Wefts: dark blue Maypole "Willamette" wool, and 2-ply white orlon.

FIGURE 12

alternating cells in the treadling (i.e., the A-block cell is woven 4 times, the B 4 times, A 4 times, B 48 times, A 4, B 4, and A 4. Therefore, the outlines do not really undulate, and the cells appear to be recesses on a plainweave ground).

Honeycomb is not exclusively a 2-block weave. Some 4-block overshot drafts adapt well to a honeycomb treadling, or a 4-block draft may be designed for the purpose. The simple diamond draft and miniature coverlet in Figure 14 illustrate the possibilities. Although a 4-block design will not have the clearly "opposite" blocks and well-defined pattern of a 2-block one, the outline wefts will still pack down in the unwoven areas and undulate around the cells (the undulation is not shown in the drawdown of Figure 14a, but it will happen when the draft is woven and removed from the loom).

13a. A sketch diagram of honeycomb weave. The "outline" threads pack down into the unwoven areas and detour around the woven cells.

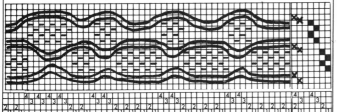

A diamond (Rosepath profile) threading draft for miniature honeycomb:

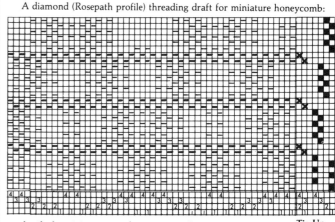

13b. A miniature honeycomb coverlet woven on the "Monk's Belt" threading of Figure 11b. This sample was woven with a colored cell weft to show the cells better against white warp and outline weft.

FIGURE 13

detail of a miniature coverlet woven on above threading:

Tie-Up
(Sinking
Shed)

Warp: white sewing thread
Sett: 30 e.p.i. (cells weave weft-faced at this sley).
Wefts: beige sewing thread cell-weft (8 shots each cell) and 2-ply white orlon outline weft.

FIGURE 14

COVERLETS: CRACKLE WEAVE

The crackle weave is *not* a traditional American coverlet weave; it was taken from Swedish techniques and promoted in the U.S. in the early 20th century by Mary Atwater. Nonetheless, because of its regularly-tied-down wefts with no weft skips longer than 3 threads, crackle is a weave which is useful for weaving miniatures. Careful drafting can yield patterns which strongly resemble traditional ones of other weaves.

Crackle is a twill derivative weave. Each block repeat is a 4-thread unit of point twill which pivots above and below one shaft (i.e. A = 1, 2, 1, 4; B = 2, 3, 2, 1; C = 3, 4, 3, 2; D = 4, 1, 4, 3). Accurate and perfect drafting of crackle weave requires following several rules; these may be found in Berta Frey's *Designing and Drafting for Handweavers*. The traditional weaving of crackle is the same as that of overshot, with pattern threads overshooting and undershooting a plainweave ground. Figure 15 shows the traditional structure of a crackle pattern. Unlike overshot, the crackle pattern wefts are always tied down every fourth thread, and two adjacent blocks always weave together (that is, the A block always weaves with either the D or the B block; B always with either A or C; etc.).

Figure 16 gives a simple 3-block profile draft and its translation into a crackle threading. The pattern has a border, and treadled as it is in the miniature coverlet shown it resembles a snowball and pinetree design.

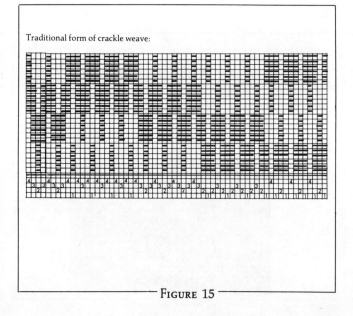

Traditional form of crackle weave:

FIGURE 15

(a): a 3-block profile draft for crackle weave:

(b): translation of (a) into crackle weave threading:

(c): both sides of a miniature coverlet woven on (b) threading.

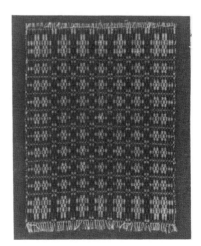

Warp: sewing thread at 30 e.p.i.

FIGURE 16

23

COVERLETS: SUMMER-AND-WINTER & VARIATIONS

Weaving a summer-and-winter fabric in miniature requires a slightly different approach from overshot, since summer-and-winter is a unit weave. One repeat of a block will always be 4 threads in this weave, and therefore variations in block size will always involve multiples of 4 threads. This has advantages and disadvantages when miniaturizing a pattern. Designing and drafting in this weave are simpler than in overshot. The step of translating the miniature profile draft into the miniature threading draft can be skipped, since summer-and-winter can be threaded on the loom directly from a profile draft by threading the proper 4-thread unit for each repeat of a block. Pattern blocks can be any width, since the pattern weft threads are "tied down" and do not skip across the entire length of the repeated block as they do in overshot.

On the other hand, classic summer-and-winter block motifs should be woven square. Four pattern shots and four tabby shots must be woven for each unit of threading; it is impossible to square a unit with that number of shots if the warp is set too closely or if the weft yarns are too heavy. A warp of sewing thread, for example, sleyed at 45 EPI will have 11¼ units per inch of width. The same thread set at 60 EPI will have more repeats per inch, but will result in rectangular or elongated patterns. Therefore, just as in weaving overshot, patterns have to be simplified and some pattern blocks eliminated.

In summer-and-winter weave, pattern threads "over-shoot" and "undershoot" a plainweave ground fabric in a path of 3/1 or 1/3 (under 3, over 1, or vice versa). The pattern has two textures formed by the predominantly weft-covered areas and the predominantly background areas (see Figure 17). The summer-and-winter fabric is usually woven using a white or light smooth thread such as cotton for the warp, the same or a slightly smaller thread for the plainweave or "tabby" weft, and a heavier, softer, colored thread such as wool for the pattern weft. Each shot of pattern weft on a pattern shed is followed by a shot of tabby weft on one of the plainweave sheds (which alternate). Every second warp thread is a tie-down thread, and they alternate; the pattern weft skips overlap in brick fashion. The warp sett is usually one that will weave a 50/50 plainweave in the background.

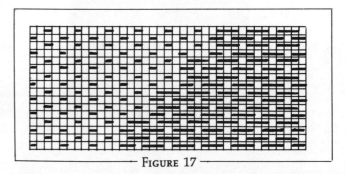

← FIGURE 17 →

24

18a. a 6-block profile draft:

18b. to translate a profile draft into summer-and-winter weave, substitute the appropriate 4-thread unit for each repeat of a block:

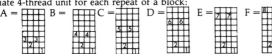

A =   B =   C =   D =   E =   F =   etc.

Therefore the above (18a) profile draft in summer-and-winter would be threaded:

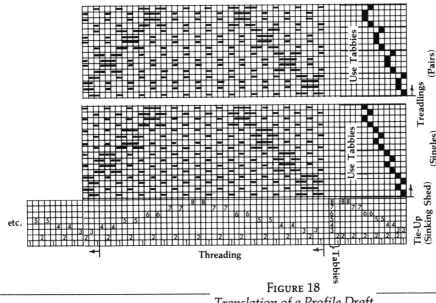

Note the standard tie-up and treadlings. The "singles" treadling was the one usually used on old coverlets. The "pairs" treadling gives an all-over pattern of tiny diamonds in background and pattern. In both treadlings, each pattern shot is followed by a tabby shot (the tabbies alternate).

FIGURE 18
Translation of a Profile Draft

As mentioned before, summer-and-winter is classified as a unit weave (that is, there are regular units of threading which are substituted for blocks in a profile draft, without reversal, modification, or added threads). Figure 18 shows the units for translating a profile draft into a threading draft in summer-and-winter weave, as well as illustrating such a translation and giving the standard tie-up and treadlings. Summer-and-winter has an additional characteristic which overshot does not have: the blocks can be woven combined as well as independently.

The simplest summer-and-winter patterns are 2-block (4-shaft) designs. Although the original old coverlets did not use this form of the weave, striking miniature coverlets can be woven on a 4-shaft summer-and-winter draft. Some of the miniatures will strongly resemble the "Patch" or "on opposite blocks" overshot coverlets. A miniature profile draft such as the "Cloudless Beauty" derivation in Figure 10b could be woven in summer-and-winter, although its 17 units per repeat (68 threads) would be a little large for 1"/1' scale.

Three other, simpler 2-block summer-and-winter profile patterns are shown in Figure 19. Draft (a) was greatly simplified from a photo of a "Mosaics" coverlet in the Henry Ford Museum. There are 5½ repeats of the 10-unit pattern across the width of the miniature coverlet. The two coverlets woven on this draft (a), folded to show both sides of each, are treadled by the standard "in pairs" treadlings;

one uses an x, y, y, x sequence of tiedowns, and the other uses y, x, x, y.

Draft 19b is a similar repeating pattern which is enough smaller (8 units) that there are 6½ repeats across the width of the miniature coverlet. Draft 19 (c) weaves a border around a large central area. The coverlets of (b) and (c) are unusual in their reversal of the standard colors: the warp and tabby weft are red and the pattern weft is white.

All of the miniature coverlets in Figure 19 are woven on warps of 24/3 cotton at 30 EPI, using sewing thread for tabby weft and fine wool or 24/3 cotton for pattern weft.

Most of the authentic old full-sized summer-and-winter coverlets were 4-block drafts, requiring a 6-shaft loom to weave. Most of the patterns were allover repeats, with no borders. Treadling was usually "in singles", not "pairs".

A weaver who wishes to weave an authentic miniature summer-and-winter reproduction will need to follow the same steps as an overshot weaver:

1. translate the threading or the fabric into a full-sized profile or block draft,
2. reduce the block draft to a miniature profile by elimination and size-cutting of blocks,
3. translate the miniature profile into a miniature threading draft (optional, since the weave can be threaded from a profile), and
4. drawdown (profile) to test the new draft.

An example of this procedure is shown in Figure 20.

19a. Profile draft and miniature coverlets adapted from "Mosaics":

19b. Another 2-block profile draft and coverlet:

19c. A 2-block profile draft with border and its coverlet:

FIGURE 19
Some 2-Block Summer & Winter Designs

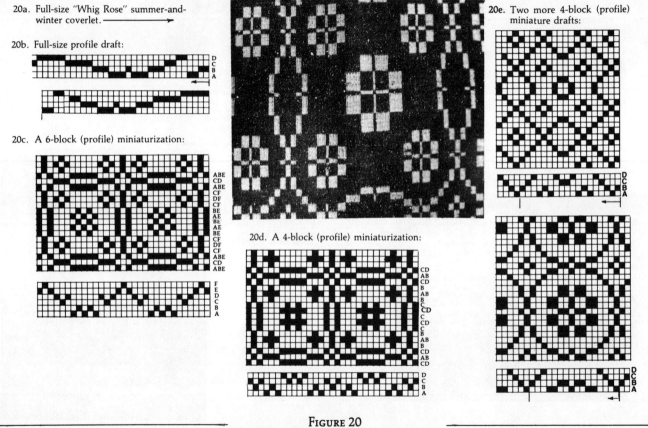

20a. Full-size "Whig Rose" summer-and-winter coverlet. ──────➤

20b. Full-size profile draft:

DCBA

20c. A 6-block (profile) miniaturization:

ABE
CD
ABE
CF
DF
CF
BE
AE
BE
AE
BE
CF
DF
CF
ABE
CD
ABE

FEDCBA

20d. A 4-block (profile) miniaturization:

CD
AB
CD
B
AB
B
C
CD
C
CD
C
B
AB
B
CD
AB
CD

DCBA

20e. Two more 4-block (profile) miniature drafts:

DCBA

DCBA

FIGURE 20
Reduction of a Summer & Winter Draft

NOTES ON FIGURE 20: In the original coverlet (a), each repeat is about one foot wide (6 complete repeats in 70" width). This means that the miniature should be about 1" repeats to appear "in scale". Since there are 22 different blocks of different sizes in a full-sized repeat (b), simple reduction to one-repeat blocks will not suffice; some blocks will have to be eliminated and the design simplified. One possible compromise is the use of more shafts, as in the 6-block profile draft (c). This is a 14-unit repeat, which is only a little larger than scale. The 4-block drafts at (d) and (e) are variations of the attempt to capture the essence of "Whig Rose" on a very small scale. The draft at (d) combines blocks in the treadling; the ones at (e) treadle blocks independently (the more authentic way of weaving summer-and-winter). None of these 4-block designs succeeds completely; each one sacrifices some element of the character of "Whig Rose" in order to capture some other characteristic element. Each of the (e) drafts is 16 to 18 units per repeat, which will weave to be about 1½ times true scale.

Since the summer-and-winter structure allows the blocks to weave independently or in any combination, a simple 6-block (8-shaft) draft such as the one in Figures 21 and 22 will allow many authentic-looking treadlings. A few such treadlings (profile) are shown.

The coverlets in Figure 22 (g) and (h) use treadlings which approximate other weaves, the "Star-and-Diamond type" and "tied doublecloth". Both of these other weaves are difficult to draft in miniature (as shown in Figure 23). Both are subject to the same problems, compromises, and limitations of draft reduction as summer-and-winter. In addition, the smallest possible unit (3-thread) in the threading weaves 5-thread skips of pattern weft when treadled, making true scale appearance difficult to achieve (see Figure 23). Typical authentic patterns in these weaves use 8 to 16 blocks, requiring 10 to 34 shafts.

Because of difficulties such as these, neither of the weaves really reduces to a tiny enough scale without losing its weave characteristics. On the other hand, a *summer-and-winter* threading provides opportunities for weaving approximations that *appear* to be woven in the two difficult weaves. Figure 24 (a) and (b) show miniature summer-and-winter treadlings which will look like miniature "Star-and-Diamond type" and "tied doublecloth" fabrics.

Several of the 2-block and 6-block miniature coverlets are shown in Figure 25 against backgrounds of a full-sized 4-block "Whig Rose" summer-and-winter coverlet and a full-sized "Star and Flower" 2-tie 3-thread-unit coverlet.

A summer-and-winter threading can also be used to weave a weft-faced 2-block coverlet such as the ones shown in Burnham, #231-234 (pp. 172-173). Figure 26 gives a small draft, to be treadled on opposites (without tabby) as shown. The warp threads will group into 3-to-1 bundles, an authentic structure for such a weft-faced coverlet. This weave can also be created on other threadings, such as miniature overshot or Monk's Belt, as described earlier.

21a. A simple 6-block profile draft (14 units per repeat):

21b. Several "Rings" and "Roses" treadlings of the draft:

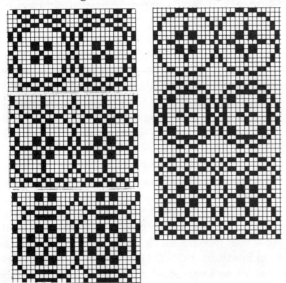

Note: most of the center motifs (on blocks D-E-F) can be used with most of the rings (sides on blocks A-B-C).

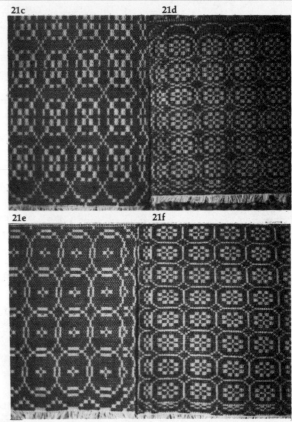

21c 21d

21e 21f

FIGURE 21

Using the same 6-block profile draft as in Figure 7, it is possible to weave a variety of other summer-and-winter motifs:

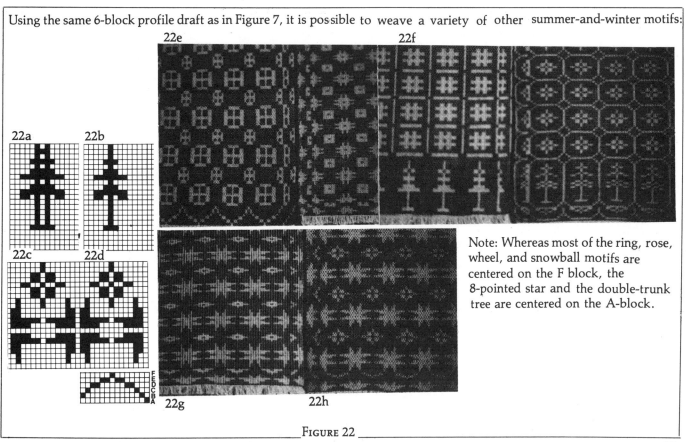

22a

22b

22c

22d

22e

22f

22g

22h

FEDCBA

Note: Whereas most of the ring, rose, wheel, and snowball motifs are centered on the F block, the 8-pointed star and the double-trunk tree are centered on the A-block.

Figure 22

23a. to translate a profile draft into the smallest form of one of the "Star and Diamond type" weaves, substitute the appropriate 3-thread unit for each repeat of a block: A=3,2,3 B=4,1,4 C=5,2,5 D=6,1,6 E=7,2,7 F=8,1,8   G=9,2,9 etc. Note that "odd" blocks must alternate with "even blocks to keep the tiedowns alternating properly. For a miniature, the draft should use only single repeats of a block, to avoid longer skips than 5 threads.

A simple 8-block point profile draft would translate into this weave as:

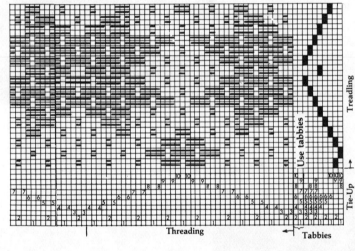

"Beiderwand" or "Tied Doublecloth" Weave in Miniature

23b. to translate a profile draft into a small version of a "Beiderwand" or "tied doublecloth" type of weave, substitute the appropriate 3-thread unit for each repeat of a block:

A=1,3,4   B=2,5,6   C=1,7,8   D=2,9,10   E=1,11,12
F=2,13,14   etc.

Note that there is no true plainweave on this threading. In full-sized originals, the tiedown threads (1 & 2) are often a different color from the rest of the warp, and are sometimes finer.

A simple 6-block point profile draft would translate into this weave as:

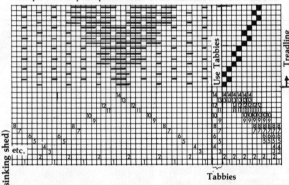

For a miniature, the draft should use only single repeats of a block, to avoid longer skips than 5 threads. In the tie-up, each block needs to be tied to a treadle with tie-down shaft 1 and to another treadle with tie-down shaft 2. Blocks may be woven independently or combined, as shown.

FIGURE 23

Treadlings on a summer-and-winter threading to appear as miniatures of other weaves:

24a. "Beiderwand" (tied double cloth)

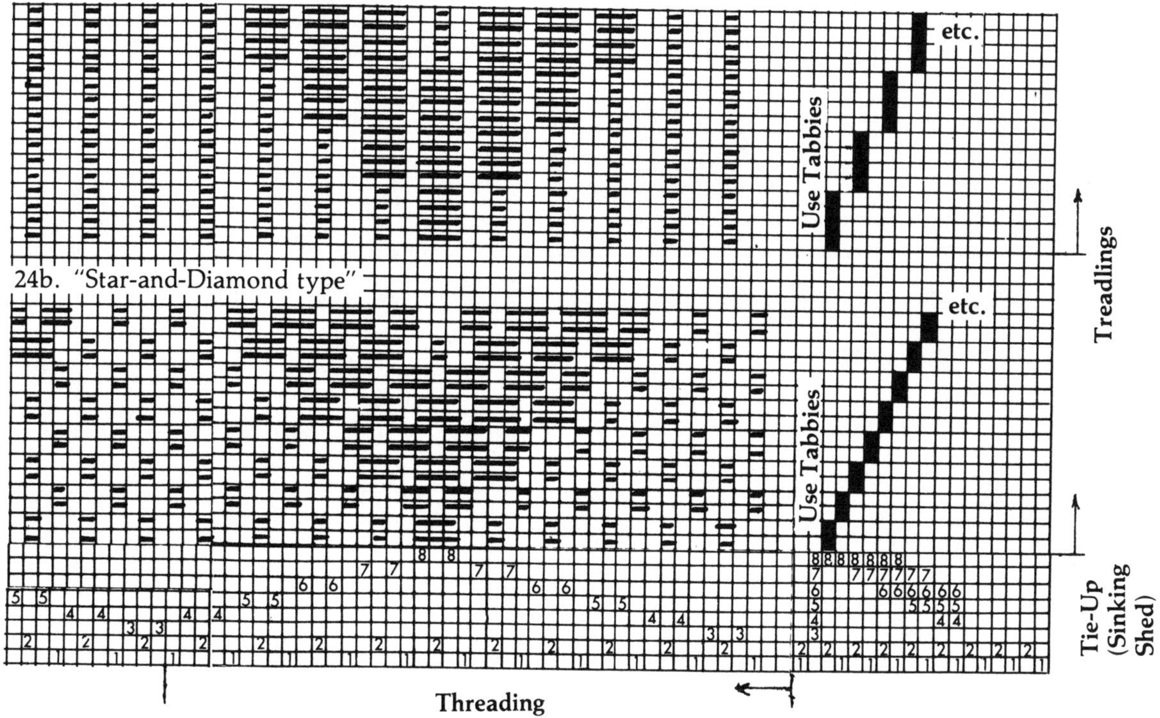

etc.
Use Tabbies
24b. "Star-and-Diamond type"
etc.
Use Tabbies
Treadlings
Tie-Up (Sinking Shed)
Threading

FIGURE 24

Summer & Winter "Imitations"

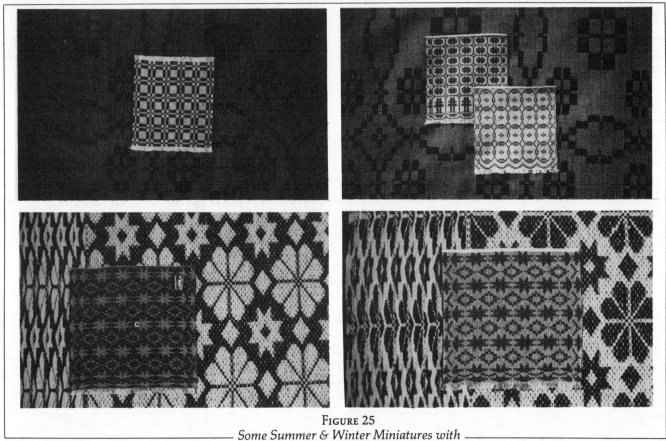

FIGURE 25
Some Summer & Winter Miniatures with
Full-Size Counterparts

A summer-and-winter threading with treadlings that will approximate a weft-faced 2-block coverlet by weaving on opposites:

To treadle, use alternating shots of:

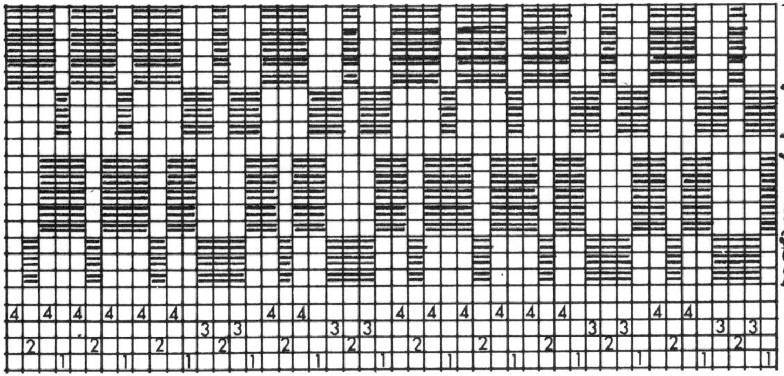

} Dark on 2-4 and light on 1-3.

} Light on 2-4 and dark on 1-3.

} Dark on 1-4 and light on 2-3.

} Light on 1-4 and dark on 2-3.

(Use *no* tabby)

FIGURE 26

COVERLETS: DOUBLE TWILL

Double twill (which Burnham calls "twill diaper" and Atwater calls "double-faced twill') is another unit weave with a 4-thread unit for each repeat of a block. Therefore, it is subject to the same miniaturization problems and limitations as summer-and-winter. In addition, this weave requires four shafts for each block, so a 4-block pattern needs a 16-shaft loom.

Double twill has no plainweave ground. Instead, the warp and pattern-weft threads interlace directly in a 1_3 and 3_1 relationship. Skips in each row of weft overlap the previous row in a diagonal (twill) direction. There are two textures, the weft-dominant (over-3-and-under-1) and the warp-dominant (under-3-and-over-1).

Figure 27a shows the standard double twill threading. One way to reduce such a pattern is to use a 3-shaft 2_1 twill for each block instead of the standard 4-shaft 3_1 draft. This will result in a 25% reduction in the size of the repeats, at the sacrifice of ⅓ of the contrast between warp-emphasis and weft-emphasis parts; it will also use 25% fewer shafts for the same block pattern (see Figure 27b-27e).

Profile drafts for original coverlets in double-faced twill are usually 4-block patterns. It is possible to reduce some profile drafts to 3-block in order to further miniaturize the double twill fabric. Some typical motifs for this weave are shown in Figure 28, along with a few suggested 3-block and 4-block profiles. Burnham illustrates 17 "twill diaper"

coverlets, Swygert shows three, and Atwater shows two in addition to many block drafts. Many of these patterns are suitable for adaptation to miniature double-faced twill.

Figure 29 shows a miniature coverlet woven on a double twill threading. At the 48 EPI setting, sewing thread weft wove flattened motifs, so a heavier (20/2 cotton) weft was used to produce the coverlet.

27a. To translate a profile draft into double twill, substitute the appropriate 4-thread unit for each repeat of a block:

A = B = C = D = etc.

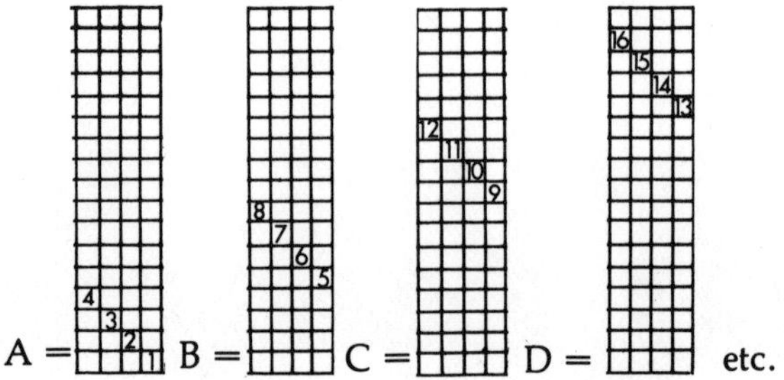

FIGURE 27A

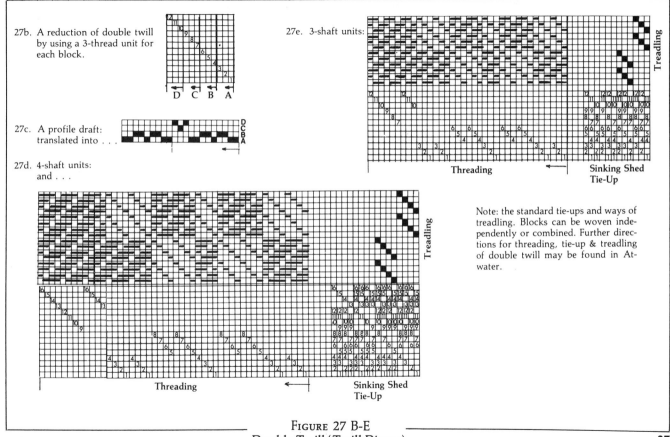

27b. A reduction of double twill by using a 3-thread unit for each block.

27c. A profile draft: translated into . . .

27d. 4-shaft units: and . . .

27e. 3-shaft units:

Threading **Sinking Shed Tie-Up** **Treadling**

Note: the standard tie-ups and ways of treadling. Blocks can be woven independently or combined. Further directions for threading, tie-up & treadling of double twill may be found in Atwater.

Threading **Sinking Shed Tie-Up** **Treadling**

FIGURE 27 B-E
Double Twill (Twill Diaper)

28a. Some profile drafts and drawdowns for typical double twill motifs:

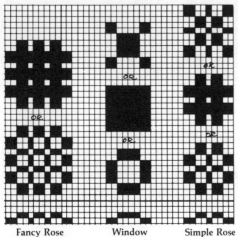

Fancy Rose or Snowball	Window or Square	Simple Rose or Star

28b. A 2-block draft adapted from a double twill coverlet,

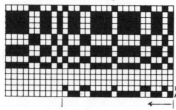

28c. A few 3- and 4-block drafts suitable for double twill miniature coverlets.

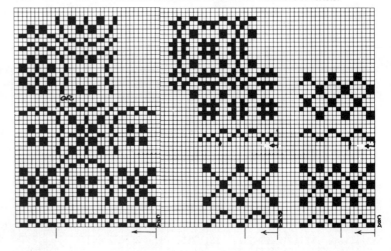

FIGURE 28
Profile Drafts For Double Twill

COVERLETS: DOUBLEWEAVE

Doubleweave, like many of the other coverlet weaves, requires a multi-shaft loom, with 4 shafts needed for each pattern block. Original full-scale coverlets usually used 4- or 5-block patterns, with a few using 6- or 8-block drafts.

Doubleweave in a geometric design is the most complex of the handwoven coverlet weaves. Two complete sets of warp and weft are used; each interlaces in a plainweave fabric. The pattern is formed by the counterchange of the two fabrics with each other from one surface of the coverlet to the other.

Although each doubleweave block requires a 4-thread unit, each surface of the fabric uses only two of those threads, so block repeats are half the size of those in the other 4-thread unit weaves previously considered. In theory, warp threads should be sleyed twice as closely for doubleweave as they would have been for a 50-50 plain-weave fabric. In practice, it was found that 90 EPI sett for polyester size 50 sewing thread was too closely sleyed to weave square. A sett of 80 EPI was better, although the fuzziness of the polyester thread at that sett necessitated hand opening of the shed.

Traditionally, most full-sized doubleweave coverlet warps were wool (blue) on one surface and cotton (white) or cotton and wool (white and red) on the other. The same yarns were used for wefts, with the wool warp and weft interweaving to form one surface and the cotton (or cotton

detail
Woven by Charleen Arnold

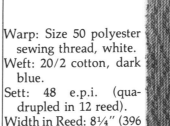

Warp: Size 50 polyester sewing thread, white.
Weft: 20/2 cotton, dark blue.
Sett: 48 e.p.i. (quadrupled in 12 reed).
Width in Reed: 8¼" (396 ends; 99 blocks).

| 9 Blocks | 21 Blocks | Border |

Border, 21, 9, 21, 9, 21, Reversed Border

Two slight revisions of the above block draft would change its appearance somewhat: a reduction of the C and D blocks from 3 repeats to 1 makes the design more compact and allows 3½ repeats of the entire pattern: inverting the border will "close" the outline of the pattern inside the parallel lines.

FIGURE 29
A Miniature Double Twill Coverlet

39

30a. A 2-block profile draft:

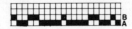

30b. Draft 24a translated into threading for doubleweave:

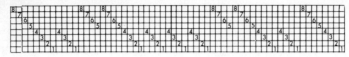

30c. Tie-up (sinking shed) for draft (b):
Each set of four treadles should be treadled in twill order with the dark and light wefts alternating, as indicated. Each sequence of 4 may be repeated as desired.

Note, the left set of four will weave dark on top in the "A"-block area; the right set will weave dark on top in the "B" area.

30d. A simple 4-block profile draft:

30e. Draft 24d translated into threading for doubleweave:

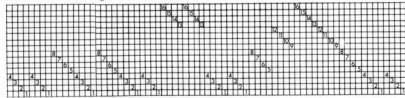

30f. Notes on tie-up: since dark threads are threaded on odd-numbered shafts and light on even-numbered in this threading, the following (sinking shed) tie-up within each set of four shafts will weave that block:

 Dark on top surface and light on bottom.
LDLD wefts, in sequence.

 Light on top surface and dark on bottom.
LDLD wefts, in sequence

FIGURE 30

Miniature Doubleweave

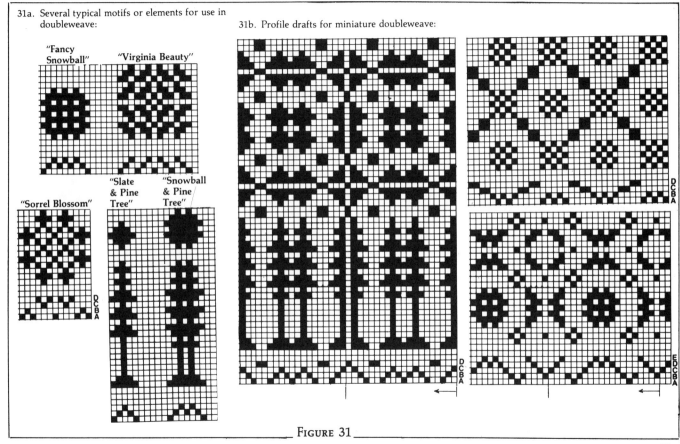

31a. Several typical motifs or elements for use in doubleweave:

"Fancy Snowball"

"Virginia Beauty"

"Sorrel Blossom"

"Slate & Pine Tree"

"Snowball & Pine Tree"

31b. Profile drafts for miniature doubleweave:

FIGURE 31

41

and wool) interweaving to form the other. Because of fuzzing problems and dense sett, a miniature doubleweave coverlet should use sewing thread (size 50 or 60 cotton, if possible) for all of the warps and wefts.

A profile draft for a 2-block (8-shaft) doubleweave miniature is shown in Figure 30a. It is the same draft as the one given for double twill in Figure 28b, and the threading is the same except that, for doubleweave, the threads should be alternately dark and light. At 80 EPI, one repeat of this pattern will be 1" across.

Figure 32d-f shows a 4-block profile draft and its threading translation, with some notes of tie-up for multi-block doubleweave. The tie-ups given are sinking shed; to weave the same threading face up on a rising shed loom, use the opposite tie-up (i.e., tie to *raise* the shafts not tied in this draft).

Several other small 2-block profile drafts are given on p. 215 of Atwater's *Shuttle-Craft* . . . . A weaver with a 12- or 16-shaft loom can use some of the smaller of Atwater's 3- or 4-block profile drafts (although many will be too large and complex for miniatures). The profile drafts already given in this book for overshot, summer-and-winter, and double twill are also suitable for miniature doubleweave. Figure 31a suggests some other miniaturized motifs typical of doubleweave, and 31b shows some combinations of motifs into complete repeats of profile patterns. Figure 32 shows a miniature doubleweave coverlet. The weaver should be warned that using these patterns in fine thread on a 16-shaft table loom is time-consuming weaving; creation of a miniature doubleweave coverlet may take as much as 1½ hours per inch!

42

A miniature doubleweave coverlet woven from the "Pine Tree and Snowball" profile draft in Figure 31b.

Woven by Charleen Arnold

Warps and Wefts: Size 50 polyester sewing thread (dark blue and white)
Sett: 80 e.p.i. (40 each surface)
Pine Tree and edge borders have been added on sides in threading.

—— FIGURE 32 ——

RUGS

RUGS: INTRODUCTION

FLOOR RUGS are another distinctive textile which can be hand woven in miniature for a dollhouse or miniature setting. Authenticity of period, design, and scale of a rug will contribute a great deal of atmosphere to such a setting. For example, a look at 17th and 18th century dollhouses of today might give the impression that most American homes of that historic period had Oriental carpets on all of their floors. But, in reality, only a small percentage of the population, the wealthy land-owners and merchants, could have afforded such things. Even today, in restorations of these fine full-sized homes, there will be a warp-faced striped rug on the floor as well as a coverlet on the bed. American handweaving flourished for 200 years after the settlers arrived; most households produced all of their own clothing, bedding, and linens. Those items that were not worn out were handed down to the next generation; those that did wear out were cut into strips and used for braided, hooked, or woven rugs. Many of these authentic handwoven items can be produced in miniature, and will be appropriate in a period room.

In like manner, a miniature rya or krokbragd rug will authenticate the appearance of a miniature room furnished in Danish Modern, whereas an American Southwest-type flatweave rug will be appropriate with the tiny Hopi and Santa Clara bowls and Papago baskets produced by today's Indian craftsmen (Figure 33).

44

Interior views of "The Trading Post", an inch-to-the-foot scale miniature of a contemporary gallery of American Indian and Eskimo crafts. The two rugs are "Chimayo-type", dark red, brown, black, and white wool in plainweave on a white cotton warp which is exposed as end fringes. All of the bowls and baskets are authentic Indian products, as are the soapstone and ivory carvings.

———— FIGURE 33 ————

As much care for scale and propriety should be used in the design, creation and choice of a miniature rug as would be used in the design, creation, and choice of a full-scale rug or any other furnishing.

RUGS: PLAINWEAVE, BALANCED

The most popular rug of all times in America has been the balanced plainweave rug which recycles strips of cloth as weft on a strong warp, or, in other words, the "rag rug". The weaving of the rag rug originated in Colonial times when every scrap of fabric was precious and needed to be used and reused. The familiarity of the rag rug continued through the 19th century, although it waned somewhat during the period of prosperity (and availability of manufactured carpeting) before World War I. The rag rug had another surge of popularity in the 1930's and 40's in the U.S., when every little town, it seemed, had at least one "rug weaver" who would create the utilitarian "hit-and-miss" patterned throw rugs for kitchen and bathroom from cotton carpet warp and strips of housedress and work-shirt fabric. Even today, despite competition from sleazy, inexpensive imported rugs in the discount stores, a strong, colorfast, machine-washable handwoven rag rug will command a better price per square foot and quicker sale than some "artistic" weaving! It is fitting, therefore, that these chapters on miniature rugs begin with the versatile and ubiquitous rag rug.

To weave a "rag" rug in miniature, the only reduction which is needed is in the size of materials used. For warp, any fine smooth yarn (such as 20/2, 20/3, 16/3, or 10/2 cotton) may be used. The warp may be a plain color, a plain color with narrow stripes near the selvedges, stripes of colors, or a random mixture of colors.

For weft, tiny strips of very fine non-ravelling cotton fabric may be used, although these will tend to make the rug thicker than true scale. Yarn is a better weft; 8/4 cotton "carpet warp" is a suitable smooth weft for a warp sett of about 12 EPI. A textured yarn (such as a fine ratine) will weave a slightly textured rug on a fine (20/2) warp. A technique may be borrowed from the Scandinavians, and several very fine threads (such as 20/2 cotton or various sewing threads) may be grouped and used as weft. If this bundle is twisted (plied) in one direction, the dark and light threads of the twist will appear as diagonal lines in the rug, resembling the Shaker twisted weft technique (see Figure 34).

Weft in authentic rag rugs may be plain color, plain with bands near the borders, or equal-sized bands alternately dark and light (since bright and light colors "advance" and dark and dull colors "recede" visually, the light bands will appear wider). Weft may also be bands of mixed colors and widths, or may be an all-over mixed "hit-and-miss" as

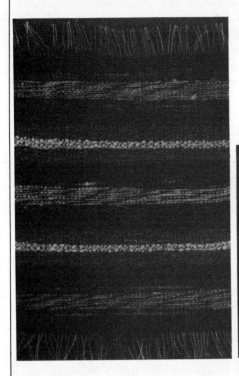

"Shaker-style" miniature rug.
Warp: 20/2 cotton in mixed colors.
Sett: 30 e.p.i.
Weft: gray, red, white, and mixed colors of
       bouclé and fine cottons

Striped & banded rugs on a warp of 16/2 cotton (CUM) striped for Stewart tartan, and plain white 16/2 mercerized cotton.
Sett: 30 e.p.i.
Wefts: 16/2 cotton.

Banded rugs.
Warp: 20/2 white cotton
Sett: 24 e.p.i.
Weft: various colors of 8/4 cotton, "Carpet warp"

FIGURE 34
Miniature Balanced Plainweave Rugs

though using up small scraps of fabric in random combination. *Rug Weaving For Everyone* by Tod and Del Deo is a source for more suggestions for well-designed rag rugs to be duplicated in miniature.

Since real rugs vary greatly in size, there is no standard size for a miniature rug. Rag rugs are usually rectangular, with an approximate proportion of 1-to-1½ or 1-to-2 (or longer, for a hall-runner, stair-carpet, etc.). Sizes of 2½" x 4", or 3" x 5", are common.

End finishes on a "rag rug" are usually either machine-sewn stay-stitching and a straight warp fringe, or over-hand-knotted warp fringe. If the end is to be machine stitched, a stick or strip of folded paper the width of the fringe-length should be woven into the warp at the end of the rug, followed by more weaving (or by another fringe stick for the beginning of the next rug). The stick or paper will hold the previous rug wefts in place until stitched; it can then be removed and the fringe can be trimmed and the rugs cut apart. If the fringe is to be hand knotted, sufficient warp length (at least 3 or 4 inches) must be left for "maxiture" fingers to tie. Hems are not recommended, as they tend to be bulky finishes, and not authentic on a rag rug. Hand hemstitching on the loom is certainly possible (although time-consuming) and will give a nice finish to an important rug.

Since a rag rug need not have a selvedge on the sides,

"mass production" of miniature rag rugs is possible by weaving on a wider warp, carefully machine stitching alongside warp threads to stay-stitch the sides too, and cutting apart close to the machine stitching.

What could be more appropriate for an American-style miniature house than a handwoven, custom-fitted rag stair- or hall-carpet?

RUGS: PLAINWEAVE, LOG CABIN

Another balanced plainweave rug weave is log cabin, so called because the design is formed of stripes that crisscross each other like logs in a cabin. The examples shown in Figure 35 were woven on a warp of 20/3 cotton sett at 24 EPI. Comparable wools were used for weft.

In log cabin, the 1/1 alternation of two colors of warp thread will weave warpwise or weftwise pin-stripes when treadled for plainweave using the same two colors alternately in the weft. The vertical stripes of pin-stripes are made to shift from warpwise to weftwise (or vice-versa) by threading two threads of the same color in succession, shifting the alternate color of warp to the opposite shed. Horizontal bands of pin-stripes are made to shift by weaving two shots of the same color in succession, shifting the alternate color weft to the opposite shed.

Log cabin, like other plainweaves, can be woven on a 2-shaft loom. The colors used are usually compatible but

47

A = dark, light 7x
B = light, dark 7x

35a. A miniature "log cabin" rug using blocks of equal size for an allover checkerboard.

35b. The two faces of a "log cabin" rug with stripes & bands forming borders.

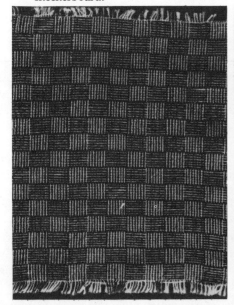
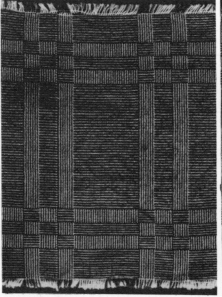

FIGURE 35
"Log Cabin" Rugs

strongly contrasted, as in the dark blue and white rugs shown in Figure 35. These rugs are suitable for any period of miniature interior. For a pre-1860 setting, the colors should be indigo blue or other natural-dye color with natural. Post-1960 settings could use a vibrant clash of colors for "op art" effect (chartreuse and electric blue, for example, or orange and "hot" pink). These rugs use the same finishing techniques as the rag rugs.

RUGS: PLAINWEAVE, WARP-DOMINANT

Balanced weave rag-type rugs are not the only use of plainweave in rugs. In an unbalanced weave, whichever element is dominant takes more wear. Therefore in American Colonial and pioneer times, a warp-dominant or warp-faced weave was sometimes used for rugs which had weaker, worn "rag" fabric strips or bundles of linen thread for weft.

The same or slightly heavier warp threads as in a miniature rag rug can be used in a miniature warp-faced rug. The only changes are a closer sett (15 to 60 EPI, depending on thread size) and a somewhat looser warp tension (to allow the warp threads to do all the curving over and under the straight wefts). Warp threads are usually in stripes. The wefts can be the same as in a miniature rag rug or can be a little stiffer (but not scale-distortingly thicker). Weft can be a plain color identical to that of the selvedge stripe, or, in a warp-dominant rug where they will show slightly, can be in bands of two or more colors. Finishing techniques can be the same as in a "rag rug".

Figure 36 shows several warp-dominant and warp-faced miniature rugs. The "Mt. Vernon" rug is stripes of black, maroon, light blue, and cream fine cotton threads. The "Homestead" rug is stripes of brown, rust, orange, and tan wool. Both are modelled after authentic old rugs; both are finished with straight warp-fringe. The widely striped rug uses coarser yarns, but it is not too thick for scale, since a wider sett has been used, making the rug warp-dominant but not warp-faced. This rug uses a 2-ply perle cotton in stripes of rust and stripes of mixed tones of cream, tan, and pink in the warp. The wefts are bands of green six-strand floss and of coral 2-ply fine cotton (the green and coral are the same *tone* and therefore do not show in the black-and-white photograph). The warp-fringe has been tied in overhand knots of four threads. "Mt. Vernon" would be suitable in a late Colonial or French interior, "Homestead" would be appropriate for a cabin, and the third rug would be fitting for any casual interior, regardless of period.

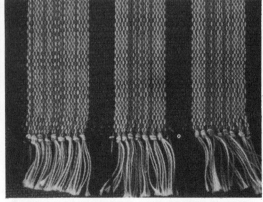

Far left: "Mt. Vernon" rug, fine cottons (including sewing thread) at 60 e.p.i. *Left:* "Homestead" rug, fine wools at 60 e.p.i. *Below:* Striped rug with knotted fringe, designed and woven by Bessie Stowall. Perle cotton at 30 e.p.i.

FIGURE 36
Three Warp-dominant Plainweave Rugs

RUGS: PLAINWEAVE, WEFT-DOMINANT

Weft-faced plainweave rugs have become more popular since the selective breeding of sheep and the development of industrial spinning and modern marketing have made firm wool rug yarns widely available. The weft-faced techniques on plainweave or on twill derivative threadings will weave most of the American Southwest (Indian and Spanish), Scandinavian, and contemporary flatweave rugs. Weft-pile rugs can be woven on a weft-faced ground on the same threadings.

Warp threads for a miniature weft-faced rug should be fine, smooth, and strong (such as 20/2, 20/3, 16/3, or 10/2 cotton). The sett should be a little wider than for balanced plainweave (10 to 20 EPI, depending on fineness of thread), and tension should be even and firm. Weft yarns may be fine wools (such as 2/20) or comparable soft, fairly smooth yarns, fine enough to pack down and cover the warp threads.

The indispensible handbook for a serious producer of rugs (full-sized *or* miniature rugs) is Peter Collingwood's *The Techniques of Rug Weaving.* Many of the weaves and finishing techniques in that book can be used for miniatures simply by executing them in fine yarns. Shown in Figure 37 are a full-sized rug-techniques sampler and its miniature replica, both woven almost entirely *a la* Collingwood.

The lower bands on the two rug technique samplers in Figure 37 are plainweave variations. Figure 38a shows this portion of the miniature sampler in closer detail. Many of these plainweave techniques can be combined to create a rug in the tradition of the American Southwest. Solid color bands, weftway stripes, warpway or pick-and-pick stripes, meet-and-separate techniques, and tapestry varieties are all appropriate for authentic-looking rugs. Several Indian-style rugs are illustrated in Figure 38. All were loom-woven, using fine cotton (10/2 or 16/2) at 12 or 15 EPI as warp, and fine wools or wool/synthetic blends (single, doubled, or tripled) as wefts. Colors are brick red, black, heather, gray, cream, and earth tones of yellow, orange, and brown, approximating natural dyes in hue.

Many end finishes are possible on these miniature rugs. A "Chimayo-type" with warp fringe can be machine stay-stitched or can use one of the weft-protector finishes (Collingwood, pp. 481-491). The rug in Figure 38c has such ends. Short of weaving a miniature rug on a miniature Navajo loom, there is no way to get the true 4-selvedge edges, but the look can be imitated by using a needle to weave each warp end back into the web after the rug has been cut from the loom.

Since Southwest-style rugs became popular and widely available only in the later part of the 19th century, their use is not appropriate in a Colonial, Federal, European, or elegant setting. In miniature, they do add immeasurably to

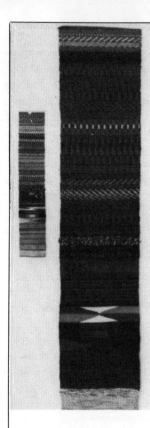

Large Sampler:
  Warp: 8/4 cotton "carpet warp".
  Sett: 4 pairs per inch.
  Wefts: various rug wools, knitting worsted,
    and similar wools.
  Size: 12" x 58"
  Threading: straight twill.

Miniature:
  Warp: 10/2 mercerized cotton.
  Sett: 12 e.p.i.
  Wefts: various fine (2/20) wools, including
    Maypole "Willamette", some doubled or
    tripled.
  Size: 4" x 21".
  Threading: Straight twill.

Techniques, top to bottom (pages refer to Collingwood text):

Broken twill treadling (pp. 273-275)
  8-pick color sequence   AAABABB
  7-pick color sequence   AABBAAB
  5-pick color sequence   ABABA
  4-pick color sequences AAAA, AAAB, BBAC,
                          AAAB, AAAA
  4-pick color sequences AAAB, AABB, ABBB,
                          ABAB, ABBA

Straight twill treadling (pp. 269-273)
  12-pick color sequence   ABBAABAAABBB
  10-pick color sequence   ABBABABBAA
  9-pick color sequence   AABAABBBB
  7-pick color sequence   ABCAABB
  7-pick color sequence   AABAAAB
  5-pick color sequence   ABCBA
  5-pick color sequence   AAABB
  5-pick color sequence   ABABA
  8-pick color sequence   AABABBAB
  4-pick color sequences ABAB, AABB, AAAB
  3-pick color sequence   AAB

Surface techniques on plainweave:
  "Moorman pile", a technique of laying-in a hand-plied textured yarn in a tie-down shed, over weft-
    faced ground (see *Weaving As An Art Form*, pp. 67-69).
  Ghiordes knot pile (rya or flossa), p. 224+.
  Weft looping, partly chained (pp. 211-218).
  Soumak (p. 183+).

Plainweave:
  Slit tapestry (p. 141+). Compensated inlay (pp. 133-137). Meet-and-separate technique, 3-color (pp.
  129-130). Meet-and-separate technique (pp. 126-127). Crossed wefts (pp. 114-121). Spots (pp. 110-
  112). Warpway or pick-and-pick stripes (pp. 103-104). Weftway stripes (pp. 102-103). Twisted wefts
  (pp. 98-100). Color blending (p. 90).

FIGURE 37

A Full-sized Rug Techniques Sampler & Its Miniature Replica

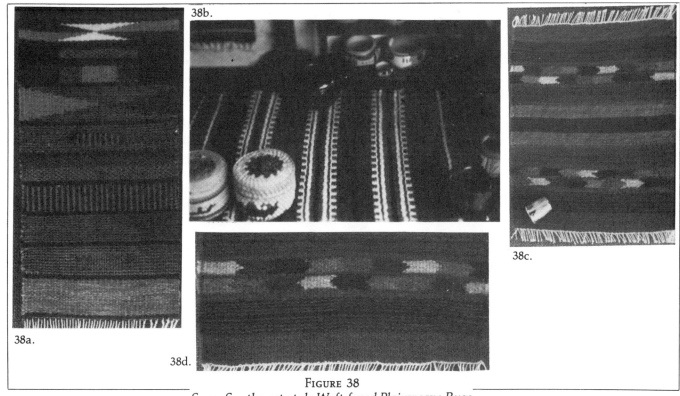

38b.

38a.

38c.

38d.

FIGURE 38
Some Southwest-style Weft-faced Plainweave Rugs

53

the look of an adobe dwelling, a craft gallery, a ski chalet, condominium, or other modern setting.

The four miniature rugs in Figure 39 are other examples of possibilities for weft-faced plainweave. The textured rug at 39a is simply a solid color nubby weft, weft-faced on a fine cotton warp at 30 EPI. The rugs in 39b-39d are the same warp and wefts as the Southwest-style rugs in Figure 38, with the banded rugs using solid, warpway, and weft-way stripes, and the diamond design using the meet-and-separate technique. Again, these miniature rugs are suitable for any modern or "periodless" miniature setting.

RUGS: TWILL, WEFT-FACED

Although a twill weave produces a thicker rug than plainweave on any particular warp setting, it is still an excellent and versatile weave for miniature rugs. A straight twill threading (1, 2, 3, 4) can be treadled plainweave (1-3, 2-4) or straight twill (1-2, 2-3, 3-4, 1-4) or broken twill (1-2, 3-4, 2-3, 1-4) or any combination of these, for a firm, smooth fabric. Color-sequence variations on these treadlings result in an amazing variety of patterns. Figure 40 shows the straight and broken twill treadlings on the miniature rug sampler from Figure 37. Specific color sequences are listed with Figure 37.

Some of the individual samples have been expanded into the miniature rugs shown in Figure 41. All of them were

54

woven on the same warp as the sampler, a 10/2 mercerized cotton at 12 EPI, threaded straight twill. All are woven with wefts of fine wool or wool blend, and all except 41c are in soft hues or heathers that resemble natural dyes. Ends are machine stitched and warp fringed.

RUGS: OTHER WEFT-FACED MINIATURES

As long as the weft skips are small enough, other threadings than plainweave and twill can be used to weave weft-faced miniature rugs. Figure 42 presents some possibilities as idea-starters.

The rugs in Figure 42 were woven on the center portion of the warp and threading of the Monk's Belt coverlet in Figure 11 and Figure 12, using fine wool wefts and no tabby. In some respects they resemble Krokbragd, the Scandinavian 3-shaft rug weave (which could itself equally well be threaded with fine threads and woven in miniature). These Monk's Belt rugs could also be woven on a fine summer-and-winter threading by treadling one of the tie-down shafts against all the other shafts to "weave on opposites" with no tabby weft.

The saddle-blanket rug in Figure 43 was woven on the point twill draft given. A shorter point twill draft (such as rosepath) would have yielded smaller diamonds.

A saddle-blanket treadling can be used on any miniature overshot or point twill threading. A standard 2/2-shaft

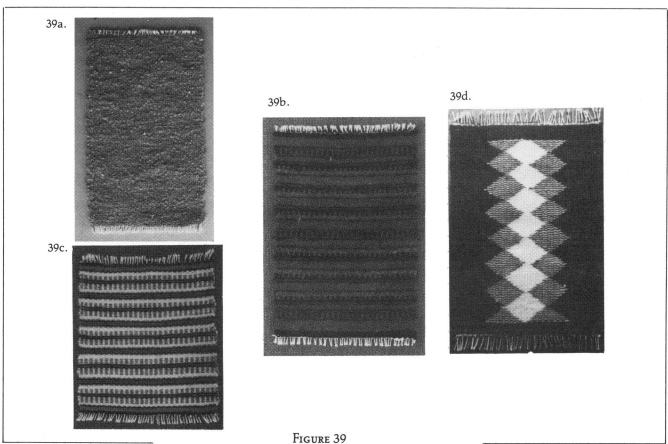

39a.

39b.

39d.

39c.

FIGURE 39
Four Contemporary Miniature Weft-faced Plainweave Rugs

55

tie-up is used. The treadling order is straight or point twill (1-2, 2-3, 3-4, 1-4 repeated or reversed). Three colors of weft are used in sequence, for example:

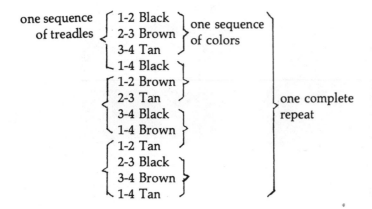

Since the number of treadles in a sequence is four and the number of colors is three, the colors shift automatically to different sheds and it takes 12 shots to complete one repeat

56

FIGURE 40
Miniature Twill Rug Sampler

41a. broken twill treadling, 4-pick color sequences.

41b. broken twill treadling, 4-pick color sequences

41c. red, white, and blue, with soldier border; broken twill treadling, 4-pick color sequences and bands of 4 or 4-multiple picks of solid. Because of many different yarns in weft making poor selvedges, sides have been machine stitched and cut to make thick weft fringe.

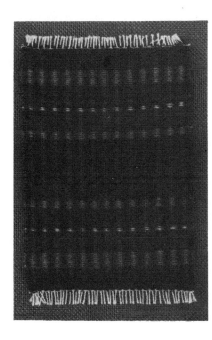

FIGURE 41

Weft-faced Miniature Rugs on a Twill Threading

of treadling. The treadling may be reversed at any point, but color sequence should be reversed simultaneously.

Authentic Indian rugs or blankets using this technique are usually woven of natural (black, brown, gray, white) or vegetal-dyed wools. The thread sizes, setts, and weft yarns given previously for miniature weft-faced rugs are also suitable for this weave. If the rug is woven to look American Southwest in style, the same limitations apply to period or era of suitable setting as applied to the plain-weave and twill "Indian" rugs.

RUGS: OTHER THREADINGS FOR FLATWEAVE

Two other flatweave rugs are shown in Figure 44 as idea-starters for the use of other weaves.

The overshot pattern in 46a is typical of the overshot "revival" in the 1930's-40's in the U.S. This example is woven on the Bertha Hayes "Domino" draft given in Figure 1. The warp and wefts are the same, with a light pattern on dark ground.

The "linenweave" rug in 44b was woven on the draft and yarns given. One miniaturist who is building an Eliza-bethan English setting claims that this rug is very similar to the full-sized one in a Shakespeare house restoration she had toured in England. Variations of such 2-tone linen weave would also be suitable for representing grass mats, jute or sisal rugs, or even a modern rug in an ultramodern "neutral" beige and tan interior with sparks of bright color in the accessories.

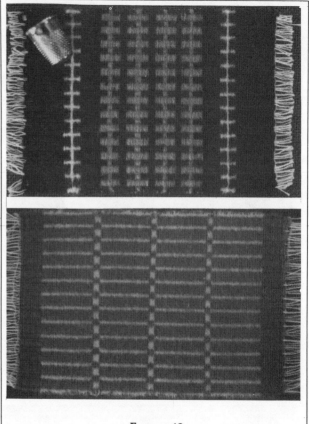

FIGURE 42
Two Monk's Belt Type Weft-Faced Rugs

43a. draft 1 Repeat

43b. Miniature rug, approx. 6" x 8", woven on above draft; cotton warp at 15 e.p.i.

43c. reverse face of b.

FIGURE 43

A Miniature Saddle Blanket Rug

RUGS: PILE TECHNIQUES

Many of the pile techniques used to weave full-sized rugs can also be used to weave miniatures, with little or no modification.

Figure 45a shows a closeup of the pile-technique segments of the full-size and miniature rug samplers from Figure 37. One of these techniques, the Ghiordes knot, was used to weave the flossa and rya miniature rugs in 47b and 47c. Both are woven on the same warp as the sampler (see Figure 37), using needlepoint wool and various fine wools and wool/synthetic blends as pile yarns. The ends are weft-faced plainweave which has been turned under and hand hemmed. Directions for weaving rya (long pile, with wide bands of plainweave between knot rows) and flossa (short pile, with closely-spaced knot rows) in the Ghiordes knot are given in Collingwood, pp. 224+.

Another pile technique which can be used in miniature is double corduroy. The same fine yarns as used in flatweave and rya rugs (10/2 cotton warp sett at 12 EPI, with fine wool weft yarns) can be used. The draft needs only slight modification to reduce the size of the skips. As shown in Figure 46, the fine wool wefts can be doubled or tripled to make a soft, full pile, and small sharp scissors are necessary for cutting the pile loops.

Pile technique rugs are not new; long "shaggy" rugs were used in early times in the very cold climates of Scandinavia

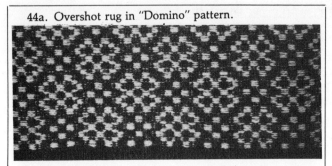

44a. Overshot rug in "Domino" pattern.

44b. Linenweave rug: Warp: 24/3 offwhite cotton
Weft: rough single-ply natural linen   Sett: 30 e.p.i.

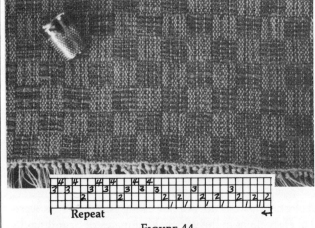

Repeat

FIGURE 44

Other Flatweave Rugs

and northern Europe as a handwoven substitute for fur bedcoverings. However, their use in bright colors and modern designs is very contemporary (1960's and beyond) in American settings; a miniature rya rug in browns and greens would be an excellent piece for a model ski lodge, and one in red and orange might be the perfect floor-covering for a dollhouse with chrome and clear plastic furniture.

RUGS: PSEUDO-PILE

In miniature it is possible to simulate a pile rug without using the time-consuming true pile techniques.

One of the easiest ways to "fake it" is to use chenille or textured (loopy) heavy yarns as weft on a plainweave or 1_3 twill threading. The loops or "fuzzies" will stick out between warp threads, forming a short pile on both faces of the fabric.

A backed fabric can be woven in the style of the Moorman technique on a straight twill threading as follows:

raise
1-3 fine smooth weft (backing)
2-4 fine smooth weft (backing)
  1 textured, loop, or bouclé weft   } one repeat of treadling
1-3 fine, smooth weft
2-4 fine, smooth weft
  3 textured weft

This treadling gives a 1_3 path to the textured yarns with a plainweave backing, making the "pile" appear only on the face of the fabric.

45a. Pile technique portions of rug samplers, showing "Moorman pile", Ghiordes knot, and weft loops.

45b. A miniature replica of a handwoven flossa rug, shown against the original. Rectangles of browns, rusts, oranges, avocado, and yellows.

45c. A miniature rya rug.

FIGURE 45
Pile Techniques

The rug in Figure 47 is woven in this manner, but on a true Moorman threading.

Supplementary warp loops can also be used to weave a miniature pile-type rug. The warp can be Maypole "Willamette" wool or a comparable size of cotton, sleyed at 20EPI and threaded on shafts 1 and 2. The supplementary warp yarns can be larger, can be novelty yarns, or can be a mixture of yarns; they are threaded on shafts 3 and 4. Since there will be far more take-up in the supplementary warp than in the ground warp, the two sets of threads must be put on the loom separately. If the loom does not have a second warp beam, the pile warp can be hung over the back beam with weights. The ground warp should be threaded on shafts 1 and 2 and beamed first, leaving empty heddles on shafts 3 and 4 at the proper places. This warp can sit on the loom at loose tension while the supplementary warp is threaded through the empty heddles left for the purpose. With both warps tied to the front beam, the supplementary threads should be gathered at the back of the loom and tied in bundles about 1" wide. The bundles can be pulled to correct tension, weighted lightly, and allowed to hang from the back beam. When both warps are sleyed together, the sett is 4 per dent in a 10 reed.

To weave a miniature pile rug on this supplementary warp setting, lift shafts 1 and 2 alternately to weave the ground fabric, and lift either shaft 3, shaft 4, or both together to raise the supplementary threads. With the pile threads raised, insert a small rod, dowel, or knitting needle (size 4) between raised threads and web. With the rod in place, weave at least 2 picks of ground fabric. A second rod can be inserted for the next row of loops, etc., until about 4 rows of loops have been woven, when the first rod can be removed and used for the next row. It will take approximately one yard of supplementary warp to weave about 5 or 6" of pile.

Miniature double corduroy rug on the loom, showing cut and uncut loops. Scissors are about 5" long.

Draft for miniature double corduroy, reduced from Collingwood p. 399. Treadling and color-shifting techniques are same as full-sized.

FIGURE 46
Double Corduroy Rug

47a. Moorman Technique.
    Warp: 2-ply natural ramie, with 20/2
       pink-beige cotton tiedowns
    Threading:
      1 Repeat:

  Wefts: Pseudo pile: rust brushed acrylic,
      orange loop mohair, and thick
      variegated yellow acrylic bouclé.
      Backing: white 10/2 cotton.
    Treadling (rising shed):
      1-3 backing ⎫
        3 pseudo pile ⎬ *one repeat*
      2-4 backing ⎪
        4 pseudo-pile ⎭

47b. Supplementary warp loops. →
    Threading:

 or or

Treadling (rising shed):
  1 ground weft
  2 ground weft
  3-4 rod

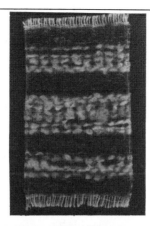

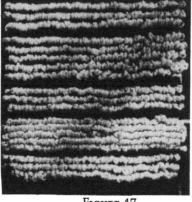

FIGURE 47
Pseudo-Pile Rug

CONTEMPORARY

INTRODUCTION

IN THE AREA OF FURNISHINGS for the modern miniature home or setting, a weaver can "let loose" with imagination and fine threads to create a wide variety of contemporary things. Whereas the weaver desiring authenticity in a miniature 19th century coverlet is bound by the limitations of historical facts, the weaver of up-to-date 1970's miniature textile furnishings can give free rein to creative ideas. This is true especially of woven wall-hangings, where the full-sized originals may be anything from fine silk and brushed mohair overshot in "fluorescent" colors to an immense free-form sculpture of jute rope.

Since the 1960's and 1970's have been decades of "The Large and The Instant", ordinary small threads such as 10/2 and 20/3 cotton and 2/20 wool will often do well for miniature works of contemporary textile art. Where a full-sized off-loom wall piece would be woven with large yarns to occupy an entire wall, the miniature can be woven with texture or color to be several inches in each dimension.

Many weaving techniques can be adapted to weaving in miniature, in addition to the weaves already shown for coverlets and rugs. This section presents a variety of "idea-starters", intended only as suggestions for further exploration, and not as a comprehensive guide to the possibilities.

CONTEMPORARY: WEAVER-CONTROLLED DESIGNS

A simple start to the weaving of contemporary miniatures is an off-loom piece. Figure 48a shows a small (1¾" x 3") three-dimensional "branch" weaving with tassels. A large blunt needle can be used as "shuttle" for such a piece. The possibilities are limited only by the size and shape of the twig and the creativity of the weaver.

Modern openweave curtains can be woven on a plain-weave or straight twill threading, or, like the deceptively simple fabric in Figure 48b, on a small overshot draft. In the curtains shown, each shot of colored weft on a pattern shed is followed by a tabby shot (on alternating tabby sheds). The wefts are laid gently into place with the beater (but not beaten), to give the open effect. Miniature curtains in dollhouses are often made from full-sized fabrics which do not drape or hang in a realistic manner; for a modern setting, handweaving a loose-weave fabric such as this from very fine threads offers an opportunity to make curtains or draperies which look to be in scale.

Weaver-controlled pickup techniques can be used in miniature, too (usually by using fine threads, appropriately sleyed). The little (1½" x 4") "Framed Latin Cross" wall hanging in Figure 49a was a beginner's project several years ago. Woven on a Rosepath threading, it has rows of 2/2 leno lace between bands of diamonds, and the cross and its frame are Brooks Bouquet technique. These same

48a. A miniature 3-dimensional "branch" weaving on a 3-pronged dry twig. "Warp" is small white cotton ratine. "Wefts" include warp yarn in addition to fine rust and tan wools.

48b. "Modern" curtain fabric.
Warp: 20/2 natural cotton
Sett: 30 e.p.i.
Wefts:
    Tabby: same as warp.
    Colors: very fine single-ply olive-green silk with yellow nubs, and fine thick-and-thin yellow & orange rayon/silk.

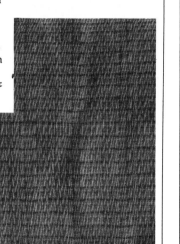

FIGURE 48

Some "Modern" Weavings

49a. "Framed Latin Cross" miniature wall hanging.
Warp: 16/3 natural cotton.
Sett: 36 e.p.i.
Weft: Same as warp.
Threading: Rosepath.

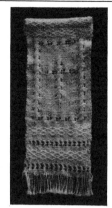

49b.
Doubleweave miniature hanging with leno lace over solid.
Warp: Size 50 sewing cotton, blue and white.
Sett: 75 e.p.i.
Wefts: Same as warps.
Threading: Straight twill.

FIGURE 49

Pick-up Lace

techniques could be used in brightly-colored sewing thread to weave miniature replicas of the Mexican burlap "drawn-thread" hangings so popular in the 1960's.

Doubleweave on a 4-shaft loom will *not* yield the exciting multi-block patterns of the coverlet drafts, but it *does* offer possibilities. Figure 49b shows a doubleweave hanging woven in the manner of the Mexican pieces mentioned above. The dark and light layers of the double cloth are interchanged to weave solid color bands, and at intervals the top surface is twisted into 3/3 or 6/6 leno over a solidly woven background. Finishing techniques used on this piece are hemstitching (top) and overhand knotting (bottom).

Fine threads can also be used to weave doubleweave pickup designs such as the one shown in Figure 50a. This Finnweave portrait of Beethoven was designed originally for a 13″ x 19″ hanging for entry in a "Beethoven's birthday greeting" contest. To weave the miniature, the same graphed design was used; the only change was in the size of thread. Size 50 cotton sewing thread at 75 EPI produced the miniature (3½″ x 6″) portrait. Directions for weaving Finnweave can be found in Tidball's monograph, *The Double Weave, Plain and Patterned*.

68

Experience in weaving Finnweave in this scale indicates several suggestions:

1. Use two strongly contrasted (but not clashing) colors,
2. use cotton thread, not polyester (the latter will fuzz and "grab" at such a close sett),
3. do not attempt to use black or very dark thread, and
4. work in a well-lighted place (a swing-arm lamp directly over the warp is ideal).

Following these suggestions will help the weaver overcome the difficulty of seeing the sewing thread warp to pick up pairs and weave the design without error.

Another weaver-controlled technique which can be used for miniatures is half-dukagang. Figure 50b shows a hanging (3½″ x 4″) which was woven with a pattern weft of four fine and bouclé yarns used together to give a variegated and textured motif on black plainweave ground. Use of very fine threads (such as sewing thread for warp and tabby, and 20/2 cotton for pattern) would yield delicate inlay patterns for table runners, hand-towels, etc. The finger-manipulated plain weaves chapter of Black's *New Key to Weaving* gives clear directions for the Dukagang and Half-dukagang techniques.

50a. Finnweave portrait of Ludwig von
     Beethoven
     Warp: Size 50 cotton sewing thread
     Sett: 75 e.p.i. (5/dent in 15 reed)
     Threading: Straight twill (1, 2, 3, 4)
         with white on 1 & 3, blue on 2 & 4.
     Wefts: same as warps.

50b. Half-dukagang miniature hanging.
     Warp: Maypole "Willamette" wool.
     Sett: 20 e.p.i.
     Wefts: Tabby: same as warp
         Pattern: 4 small novelty yarns used
         used together.
     Threading: Straight twill.
     Tie-up: Rising shed.

     Treadling: alternate treadles A & B
         for ground; use treadle C for pat-
         tern inlay (face down).

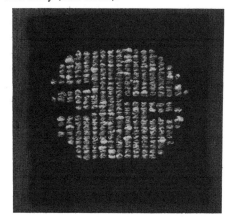

FIGURE 50
Other Pick-Up Techniques

CONTEMPORARY: LOOM-CONTROLLED WEAVES

A flamepoint treadling on overshot or point twill drafts will weave a fabric that can be either "authentic Colonial" or "op-art modern", depending on the colors used.

A standard tie-up (1-2, 2-3, 3-4, 1-4) is used. Treadling for flamepoint is straight twill, using 4 colors in sequence as in the following example:

raise shafts:

1-2 maroon	
2-3 red	repeat as many times as desired
3-4 orange	
1-4 yellow	
1-2 red	
2-3 orange	repeat as many times as desired
3-4 yellow	
1-4 maroon	
1-2 orange	
2-3 yellow	repeat as many times as desired
3-4 maroon	
1-4 red	
1-2 yellow	
2-3 maroon	repeat as many times as desired
3-4 red	
1-4 orange	

Since the number of treadles in a sequence and the number of colors are the same, each color will fall in the same shed each time the treadling is repeated. When the first color of the sequence is shifted to the bottom, each color shifts to the next shed. The more times a sequence of four is repeated before shifting, the steeper the slant of the "flame" will be.

The example in Figure 51 was intended for use as chair upholstery. The scale of the pattern fitted the chair very well, but the fabric was too heavy to turn under as hems and seam allowances. If the technique were used with even finer threads, the resulting fabric could be used on a Federal wing chair if seams could be covered with tiny braid and the chair-back could be covered with felt or something which required no turning under of the hand-woven parts. The fabric shown would make an appropriate covering for a miniature piano bench, where no curved seams are required.

MULTI-SHAFT WEAVES

Two examples of 8-shaft weaves are presented here from among the myriad possibilities.

The placemat design in Figure 52 is a somewhat more contemporary use of the traditional summer-and-winter weave from Section II. The conversion of the design from full-sized coverlet draft to full-sized placemat to miniature

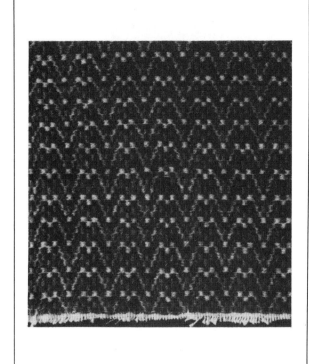

FIGURE 51

A Miniature Flamepoint Upholstery Fabric

mat is shown. Just a reduction and simplification of the coverlet design were necessary to fit the full-sized place-mat, further reduction and simplification were necessary to convert the design to the miniature placemat. The "Snow-ball" was eliminated and the "Pine Tree" was simplified to make it as small as possible without complete loss of character.

One comment is in order at this point: Almost all of the miniatures shown so far were woven on full-sized floor looms with few problems, but because this placemat warp was so narrow, the floor loom exerted too much pressure on the fine warp threads, and warp breakage happened with frustrating regularity. This problem could be over-come by warping the pattern several repeats wide with extra "selvedge" blocks threaded between repeats. The placemats could then be woven in multiples side by side and could be machine stitched and cut apart so that each mat had fringe on all four edges.

The tablecloths and samples shown in Figure 53 were all woven on an 8-shaft point twill threading. A direct tie-up (1, 2, 3, 4, 5, 6, 7, 8, 1-3-5-7, 2-4-6-8) was used so that the shafts could be raised in any combination. Most of the motifs were "drawn down" on paper first. It was found that because the repeats of threading were so small, little tie-down of the weft threads between motifs was needed. Finished cloths were hand hemmed.

What began as a profile draft for a 6-block coverlet (52a.) from Atwater, p. 44, and draft #234 was reduced from 111 units to 45 units of a 5-block draft (block F is edge, and never weaves). This was woven in Lily Frost-tone and Kentucky Yarn as a full-sized placemat (b). The draft was simplified further to draft (c) and woven of Size 60 cotton sewing thread and CUM 16/2 cotton as miniature placemats. At 48 e.p.i., the miniatures are 1½″ x 2½″.

52a.

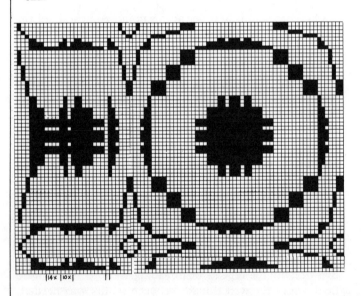

52b.

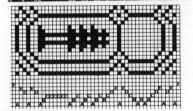

52c.

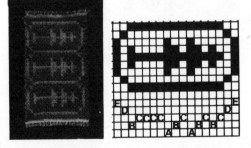

FIGURE 52
A Summer-and-Winter "Pine Tree" Design

Tablecloths and samples woven on an 8-shaft point twill threading:
  Warp: Size 60 white sewing thread (cotton)
  Threading: 8-shaft point twill
  Sett: 45 e.p.i. in 15 reed
  Wefts: tabby: same as warp
         pattern: CUM 16/2 cotton

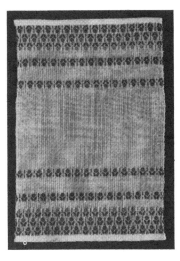

FIGURE 53
8-Shaft Point Twill Motif Borders

73

The original inspiration for these designs was 8-shaft Rosepath samples in two weavers' guild newsletters, "Valentines For You" in the *Pinellas* (Fla.) *Weaving News*, February 15, 1975, and "Spring Bouquet" in the Rocky Mountain Weavers Guild (Colo.) *Shuttle Scuttle*, April, 1974. The tablecloth and sample motifs in Figure 53 could be woven on a Rosepath threading with slight modifications. If so woven, each repeat of threading would be two threads wider, and tie-down of some of the wefts would occur automatically.

Two of the finished tablecloths were used in boxed vignettes (see Figure 54). The Valentine party is serving mints, cake, heart cookies and suckers, and punch cooled by a heart "ice-ring". The Easter sunrise, seen between draperies of the fabric of Figure 48b, glows on a breakfast of scrambled eggs, spinach quiche, hot-cross buns, and orange juice, with an egg tree, panorama eggs, and royal icing baskets decorating the table and an egg hunt awaiting the participants. The other motifs shown in the samples could easily be used in holiday settings like these for Halloween, Independence Day, St. Patrick's Day, a bridge party, etc.

FIGURE 54
Two Miniature Settings

FIGURE 55
A Fair Conclusion

CONCLUSION

The designs which we have presented in this book are intended as idea-starters and creativity-prods. They are not meant to be comprehensive statements of all that can be done. Other coverlet patterns can be miniaturized. Other rug weaves can be reduced and woven with fine threads. Other weave techniques, from weaver-controlled tapestry to draw-loom damask, can be executed in miniature by a weaver who is dedicated (crazy) enough to want to do it.

Of course, miniature craft work is not limited to weaving either. Figure 55 shows part of a 1"/1' scale Autumn Craft Fair in the Park, where the weaver has been joined by other crafters to sell crocheted rugs, quilts, tatted snowflakes, cross-stitch pictures, photographic prints, pottery, and several other categories of handcrafted objects for the miniature home. The possibilities are legion, and it is hoped that *Weaving in Miniature* has helped inspire pursuit of them.

BIBLIOGRAPHY

Anderson, Clarita and Judith Gordon and Naomi Whiting Towner, "An Analysis of Star and Diamond Weave Structures", *Shuttle, Spindle & Dyepot* Issue 36 (Fall 1978).

Atwater, Mary Meigs, *The Shuttle-Craft Book of American Hand-Weaving*, rev. ed., Macmillan, 1951.

Black, Mary E., *New Key to Weaving*, The Bruce Publishing Co., 1957.

Burnham, Harold B. and Dorothy K., *"Keep Me Warm One Night"; Early Handweaving in Eastern Canada*, Univ. of Toronto Press, 1972.

Collingwood, Peter, *The Techniques of Rug Weaving*, Watson-Guptill Publications, 1968.

Davison, Marguerite Porter, *A Handweaver's Pattern Book*, rev. ed., pub. by author, 1966, c1950.

Estes, Josephine E., *Original Miniature Patterns for Hand Weaving*, 2 v., n.p., n.d.

Frey, Berta, *Designing and Drafting for Handweavers*, Macmillan, 1958.

Moorman, Theo, *Weaving As an Art Form*, Van Nostrand Reinhold Co., 1975.

Strickler, Carol, "Landes Hybrid", *Interweave* Vol. I, No. 3 (Spring, 1976).

———, comp., *A Portfolio of American Coverlets, Number 1*, Interweave Press, 1978.

———, comp., *A Portfolio of American Coverlets, Number 2*, Interweave Press, 1979.

———, "Portraits in Double Weave", *The Weaver's Journal*, Vol. 1, No. 3 (Jan. 1977).

Swygert, Mrs. Luther M., *Heirlooms from Old Looms: A Catalogue of Coverlets Owned by The Colonial Coverlet Guild of America and Its Members*, Colonial Coverlet Guild of America, 1955.

Tidball, Harriet, *The Double Weave, Plain and Patterned*, Shuttle Craft Monograph One, The Shuttle Craft Guild, 1960.

Tod, Osma Gallinger and Josephine Couch DelDeo, *Rug Weaving for Everyone*, Bramhall House, 1957. Republished 1976 by Dover as *Designing and Making Handwoven Rugs*.